Essential Idioms in English

Phrasal Verbs and Collocations

FIFTH EDITION

ROBERT J. DIXSON

Longman

longman.com

Essential Idioms in English: Phrasal Verbs and Collocations

Pearson Education, 10 Bank Street, White Plains, NY 10606

Acquisitions editor: Virginia L. Blanford
Vice president, director of design and production: Rhea Banker
Director of electronic production: Aliza Greenblatt
Executive managing editor: Linda Moser
Production editor: Jane Townsend
Assistant editor: Tara Maldonado
Director of manufacturing: Patrice Fraccio
Senior manufacturing buyer: Nancy Flaggman
Cover and interior design: Tracey Munz Cataldo
Digital layout specialist: Lisa Ghiozzi
Text font: Meta Plus Book 11/14, Sabon 11/12
Text and cover art: George Thompson

Library of Congress Cataloging-in-Publication Data
Dixson, Robert James.
   Essential idioms in English / Robert J. Dixson.–New ed. [5th ed.]
     p. cm
   Includes index.
   ISBN 0-13-141176-4
   1. English language–Textbooks for foreign speakers. 2. English language–Idioms. I. Title.
PE1128.D513 2003
428.2'4–dc21

                                       2003044730
ISBN: 0-13-141176-4

LONGMAN ON THE **WEB**

Longman.com offers online resources for
teachers and students. Access our Companion
Websites, our online catalog, and our local
offices around the world.

Visit us at **longman.com**.

Printed in the United States of America
1 2 3 4 5 6 7 8 9 10–VHO–07 06 05 04 03

CONTENTS

Contents **V**

PREFACE

Idiomatic expressions have long played an important role in the English language. In fact, the use of idioms is so widespread that understanding these expressions is essential to successful communication, whether in listening, speaking, reading, or writing. The student may learn grammar and, with time, acquire adequate vocabulary, but without a working knowledge of such idioms as *above all, to get along, on the whole, to look up,* and so on, even the best speech will remain awkward and ordinary.

Teachers of English have long recognized that idiomatic expressions add grace and exactness to the language. The alert teacher will make their study an integral part of the teaching process. Even so, learning such expressions is never an easy task for the student learning English as a second or foreign language. Attempts to translate literally from the student's native tongue usually lead to roundabout expressions of meaning and, more often, to confusion.

For this reason, the idioms, phrasal verbs, and collocations included in this book have been selected because they are, for the most part, basic to good English—and the book is called, appropriately, *Essential Idioms in English*. Students are not burdened with a discussion of the origins of idioms, nor is there an attempt to define the exact nature of an idiom except to point out that as a phrase it has a meaning different from the meanings of its individual parts. (This essential characteristic is one reason why it is often difficult to translate an idiom from one language to another without incurring some change in meaning or usage.)

Our hope is that experienced ESL and EFL teachers will agree, for the most part, with the selection of idioms in this text. This edition has been updated to include current idioms, and older usages have been dropped. But every selection, no matter how careful, is necessarily arbitrary, because the range is so great. Our intent is to provide a useful learning and reference tool for students who want to speak appropriate, contemporary English.

NEW TO THIS EDITION

This new edition of a classic text retains its original three-section format: Beginning (Lessons 1–13), Intermediate (Lessons 14–27), and Advanced (Lessons 28–39). New idioms have of course been included, and outdated idioms have been removed throughout. Lessons in all sections review and build upon idioms introduced in earlier lessons. In some cases, notes that explain special usage or meaning are provided after the definitions, and related idiomatic forms are listed. The wide assortment of exercises provides variety in the activities from one section to another.

Essential Idioms has always included two-word, or phrasal, verbs in the general category of idioms. A *phrasal verb* is one whose meaning is altered by the addition of a *particle* (a preposition used with a verb to form an idiomatic expression.) *To look,* for example, may become *to look up* or *to look over,* each having its own special meaning. When a phrasal verb can be separated by a noun or pronoun, the symbol (S) for separable is inserted in the definition. Sentences illustrating both separable and nonseparable forms are included in the examples.

In this edition, students will also find *collocations* included in each section. Collocations are words that tend to be used together, not based on rules of grammar, but rather based on traditional patterns of usage by native speakers. Collocations can occur in a number of different patterns. Among the most common are adjective + noun *(shining star, heavy breathing),* verb + noun *(take a bus, deliver a baby),* and verb + adverb *(fully document).* The addition of collocations reflects the growing interest in these unique word patterns in second-language study.

As in the previous edition, this edition includes an Appendix that lists equivalent idioms in French and Spanish, and we have added Portuguese in this edition as well. We hope this will make *Essential Idioms* especially useful to native speakers of these languages and will provide students with a surer grasp of English idioms and greater confidence in using them.

Finally, also new to this edition is a section on Dictionary Skills, which includes a brief set of activities designed to provide students with strategies for using one of their primary language-learning tools.

Overall, this classic text continues to provide an outstanding, comprehensive introduction to idiomatic English for learners at all levels.

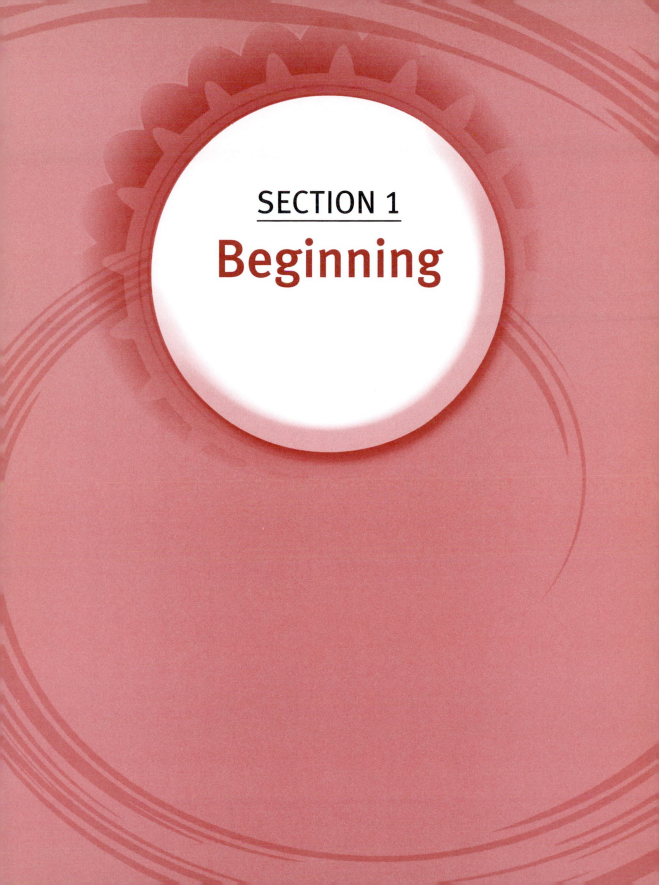

SECTION 1
Beginning

Lesson 1

to get in/to get on: to enter or to board a vehicle
To get in is used for cars; *to get on* is used for all other forms of transportation.

- It's easiest to *get in* the car from the driver's side. The door on the other side doesn't work well.

- I always *get on* the bus to work at 34th Street.

to get out of/to get off: to leave or to descend from a vehicle
To get out of is used for cars; *to get off* is used for all other forms of transportation.

- Why don't we stop and *get out of* the car for a while?

- Helen *got off* the train at the 42nd Street terminal.

to put on: to place on oneself (usually said of clothes) **(S)***

- Mary *put on* her coat and left the room.

- *Put* your hat *on* before you leave the house.

to take off: to remove (usually said of clothes) **(S)**

- John *took off* his jacket as he entered the office.

- *Take* your sweater *off*. The room is very warm.

---

*The symbol (S) indicates that on idiom is *separable*—that a noun or noun phrase may be placed between the verb and the special preposition (called a *particle*). In these cases, examples of both separable and inseparable forms are given. See the index, page 271, for further details.

---

to turn on: to start or cause to function (also: **to switch on**) **(S)**

- Please *turn on* the light; it's too dark in here.

- Do you know who *turned* the air conditioning *on*?

to turn off: to cause to stop functioning (also: **to switch off, to shut off**) **(S)**
Turn on and turn off, as well as their related forms, are used for things that flow, such as electricity, water, gas, etc.

- Please *turn off* the light when you leave the room.

- Are you really listening to the radio, or should I *turn it off*?

right away: very soon; immediately (also: **at once**)

- Dad says that dinner will be ready *right away*, so we'd better wash our hands and set the table.

- Tell Will to come to my office *right away*. I must see him immediately.

- Stop playing that loud music *at once!*

to pick up: to lift with one's fingers or hands **(S)**; to retrieve or collect **(S)**; to learn **(S)**

- Harry *picked up* the newspaper that was on the front doorstep.

- Lucia was so busy that she forgot to *pick* her son *up* from school.

- Margot *picks up* math easily, but she is not good at reading.

sooner or later: eventually, after a period of time

- If you study English seriously, *sooner or later* you'll become fluent.

- I'm too tired to do my homework now; I'm sure I'll do it *sooner or later*.

to get up: to arise, to rise from a bed; to make someone arise **(S)**
For the last definition a noun phrase must separate the verb and particle.

- Carla *gets up* at seven o'clock every morning.

- At what time should we *get* the children *up* tomorrow?

to come up with: to find, to discover

- After worrying for days, I finally *came up with* a solution to my problem.

- Even though Kwan doesn't have a job, he always *comes up with* enough money to pay his bills.

at first: in the beginning, originally

- *At first* English was difficult for him, but later he made great progress.

- I thought *at first* that it was Sheila calling, but then I realized that it was Beth.

EXERCISES

 Choose the appropriate idiomatic expression to substitute for the italicized word or words in each sentence below.

1. His alarm clock is always set for six o'clock. He *arises* at the same time every day.
   a. turns off
   b. gets up
   c. puts on

2. It's 4 P.M. now, and this important letter must be mailed today. Can you take it to the post office *immediately*?
   a. at first
   b. right away
   c. sooner or later

3. Be sure to *switch off* the light before you leave the house.

    a. to turn off

    b. to take off

    c. to get off

4. Pat *placed* her new hat on her head while looking in the mirror.

    a. picked up

    b. put on

    c. gets on

5. *Remove* your jacket and sit down for a few minutes.

    a. Turn on

    b. Get on

    c. Take off

6. I want to stay single for a while, but I hope to get married *eventually*.

    a. sooner or later

    b. right away

    c. at first

7. *In the beginning* I thought that golf was boring, but I like it now.

    a. To get on

    b. At once

    c. At first

8. He *boarded* the bus at Broadway and 79th Street.

    a. got off

    b. got on

    c. picked up

9. John *took* the pencil and began to write a note.

   a. turned on

   b. got off

   c. picked up

10. Eli finally *found* a great topic for his history report.

   a. got up

   b. came up with

   c. put on

B *Fill in each blank with the appropriate form of an idiomatic expression from this lesson.*

Every morning, Jean's alarm clock makes a loud ringing noise. She _____ the alarm clock immediately after it rings, but she doesn't get out of bed _____. She waits a few minutes before she _____.

Jean would like to stay in bed all morning, but _____ she has to get up. Then she _____ the bedroom light and goes to her closet. She _____ her pajamas and _____ her work clothes.

Lesson 2

to dress up: to wear formal clothes, to dress very nicely

- We should definitely *dress up* to go to the theater.

- You don't have to *dress up* for Mike's party.

at last: finally, after a long time

- We waited for hours and then the train arrived *at last*.

- Now that I am sixteen, *at last* I can drive my parents' car.

as usual: as is the general case, as is typical

- George is late for class *as usual*. This seems to happen every day.

- *As usual*, Dora received first prize in the swimming contest. It's the third consecutive year that she has won.

to find out: get information about, to determine **(S)**
This idiom is separable only when a pronoun is used, as in the second example.

- Will you please try to *find out* what time the airplane arrives?

- I'll call right now to *find* it *out*.

to look at: give one's attention to; to watch

- The teacher told us to *look at* the board and not at our books.

- I like to walk along a country road at night and *look at* the stars.

to look for: to try to find, to search for
An adverb phrase such as *all over* can be put between the verb and preposition, as in the second example. However, the idiom cannot be separated by a noun or pronoun.

- He's spent over an hour *looking for* the pen that he lost.

- There you are! We've *looked* all over *for* you.

all right: acceptable, fine; yes, okay
This idiom can also be spelled *alright* in informal usage.

- He said that it would be *all right* to wait in her office until she returned.

- Do you want me to turn off the TV? *Alright,* if you insist.

all along: all the time, from the beginning (without change)

- She knew *all along* that we'd never agree with his plan.

- Did you know *all along* that I'd give you a birthday present, or were you surprised?

little by little: gradually, slowly (also: **step by step**)

- Karen's health seems to be improving *little by little*.

- If you study regularly each day, *step by step* your vocabulary will increase.

to tire out: to make very weary due to difficult conditions or hard effort
(also: **to wear out**) **(S)**

- The hot weather *tired out* the runners in the marathon.

- Does studying for final exams *wear* you *out?* It makes me feel *worn out!*

to spend time: to do an activity over a period of time **(S)**

- Adrian would rather *spend time* watching TV than doing homework.

- I *spent* too much *time* getting ready this morning, so I was late for work.

never mind: don't be concerned about it; ignore what was just said

- When he spilled his drink on my coat, I said, "*Never mind*. It needs to be cleaned anyway."

- So you weren't listening to me again. *Never mind;* it wasn't important.

EXERCISES

A   *Choose the appropriate idiomatic expression to substitute for the italicized word or words in each sentence below. Idioms from previous lessons are indicated by number.*

1. Emily is *trying to find* the purse that she lost yesterday.
   a. finding out
   b. looking at
   c. looking for

2. *As is typical,* Doug is late for the meeting.
   a. At last
   b. All along
   c. As usual

3. Were you able *to determine* what his occupation is?
   a. to find out
   b. to pick up (Lesson 1)
   c. to spend time

4. I am *very weary* after all that physical exercise today.
   a. turned off (Lesson 1)
   b. tired out
   c. never mind

5. Samuel was upset earlier, but he is *fine* now.
   a. tired out
   b. as usual
   c. all right

6. John's mother knew that he wasn't telling the truth *from the beginning*.
   a. all along
   b. all right
   c. little by little

7. *Eventually*, Mario will be able to speak English better than he does now.
   a. Never mind
   b. Sooner or later (Lesson 1)
   c. At last

8. Is it *okay* for Mary to borrow our car for a few hours?
   a. right away (Lesson 1)
   b. all right
   c. step by step

9. Would you please *give your attention to* me while I'm talking?
   a. dress up
   b. look at
   c. wear out

10. They waited for forty-five minutes until *finally* the server brought their food.
   a. at last
   b. little by little
   c. at first (Lesson 1)

B *Fill in each blank with the appropriate form of an idiomatic expression from this lesson.*

BOB: Jim, should we _____ for the party tonight?

JIM: No, casual clothes are fine. I'm _____ my shoes. Have you seen them?

BOB: No. Did you check that closet by the front door?

JIM: Of course I did! Gosh, my legs hurt. I'm really

_____ from playing so much soccer today.

BOB: What did you say?

JIM: Oh, _____. It wasn't important.

BOB: Sorry, I was _____ the newspaper. There's another article about the robbery.

JIM: Have the police _____ who stole the million dollars?

BOB: No, they haven't. But they have _____ a lot of _____ looking for him.

JIM: Hey, I just found my shoes! They were in that closet

_____!

BOB: I told you so!

Lesson 3

to pick out: to choose, to select **(S)**

- Ann *picked out* a good book to give to her brother as a graduation gift.

- Johnny, if you want me to buy you a toy, then *pick* one *out* now.

to take one's time: to do without rush, not to hurry
This idiom is often used in the imperative form. (See the first example.)

- There's no need to hurry doing those exercises. *Take your time.*

- William never works rapidly. He always *takes his time* in everything that he does.

to talk over: to discuss or consider a situation with others **(S)**

- We *talked over* our ideas about redecorating the room, but we couldn't reach a decision.

- Before I accepted the new job offer, I *talked* the matter *over* with my wife.

to lie down: to place oneself in a flat position, to recline

- If you are tired, why don't you *lie down* for an hour or so?

- The doctor says that Grace must *lie down* and rest for a short time every afternoon.

to stand up: to rise from a sitting or lying position (also: **to get up**)

- When the president entered the room, everyone *stood up*.

- Don't just sit there. *Get up* and help me clean the house!

to sit down: to be seated (also: **to take a seat, to have a seat**)

- We *sat down* on the park bench and watched the children play.

- There aren't any more chairs, but you can *take a seat* on the floor.

- Please *have a seat*. The program will be starting soon.

all (day, week, month, year) long: the entire day, week, month, year

- I've been working on my income tax forms *all day long*. I've hardly had time to eat.

- It's been raining *all week long*. We haven't seen the sun since last Monday.

by oneself: alone, without assistance

- Francis translated that French novel *by himself*. No one helped him.

- Paula likes to walk through the woods *by herself*, but her brother prefers to walk with a companion.

on purpose: for a reason, deliberately
This idiom is usually used when someone does something wrong or unfair.

- Do you think that she didn't come to the meeting *on purpose?*

- It was no accident that he broke my glasses. He did it *on purpose*.

to get along (with): to associate or work well (with)

- Terry and her new roommate don't *get along;* they argue constantly.

- Adrienne has a hard time at school because she doesn't *get along* with her biology professor.

to make a difference (to): to be of importance (to), to affect (also: **to matter to**) (S)
These idioms are often used with adjectives to show the degree of importance.

- It *makes a big difference to* me whether he likes the food I serve.

- Does it *make any difference* to you where we go for dinner?
  No, it doesn't *matter to me*. It *matters* a lot *to* Liza, though. She's a vegetarian.

to take out: to remove, to extract **(S)**; to go on a date with **(S)** (also: **go out (with)**)

- Students, *take out* your books and open them to page twelve.

- Did you *take* Sue *out* last night?

- No, she couldn't *go out with* me.

EXERCISES

Choose the appropriate idiomatic expression to substitute for the italicized word or words in each sentence below. Idioms from previous lessons are indicated by number.

1. I think that you should *remove* the last two sentences in the paragraph.
   a. take out
   b. pick out
   c. talk over

2. If you *don't hurry* in completing your schoolwork, you'll do a better job.
   a. get off (Lesson 1)
   b. lie down
   c. take your time

3. Does it *affect* you if I work late tonight?
   a. get along with
   b. make a difference to
   c. pick out

4. I don't like to go to the movies *alone*.
   a. as usual (Lesson 2)

   b. by myself

   c. on purpose

5. Do you have a moment *to try to find* my keys with me?
   a. to talk over

   b. to look for (Lesson 2)

   c. to get up

6. The child said that she didn't break the window *deliberately*.
   a. on purpose

   b. all day long

   c. making a difference

7. Did you *go on a date with* your new girlfriend again today?
   a. matter to

   b. stand up

   c. go out with

8. It's cold outside; you'd better *place* a sweater *on yourself*.
   a. sit down

   b. put on (Lesson 1)

   c. take out

9. Fortunately, Marie is *associating well with* her new co-workers.
   a. tiring out (Lesson 2)

   b. talking over

   c. getting along with

10. Don't sit on the dirty ground like that; *rise* right now!
    a. get up
    b. lie down
    c. sit down

B *Fill in each blank with the appropriate form of an idiomatic expression from this lesson.*

JEAN: Hi, Pete. Did you come _____?

PETE: Yes, Sarah couldn't come. She's at the dentist's office.

JEAN: Oh? Why is that?

PETE: The dentist has to _____ one of her teeth. It has been hurting _____ week _____.

JEAN: That's too bad. Well, I'm glad you're early.

PETE: Why? I didn't come early _____.

JEAN: I know, but now we have time to _____ that problem regarding the new employee.

PETE: You mean the woman who doesn't _____ her co-workers?

JEAN: Exactly. But please, take off your coat first and _____ on the couch.

PETE: Thanks.

Lesson 4

to take part in: to be involved in, to participate in (also: **to be in on**)

- Martin was sick and could not *take part in* the meeting yesterday.

- I didn't want to *be in on* their argument, so I remained silent.

at all: to any degree (also: **in the least**)
This idiom is used with the negative to add emphasis to a statement.

- Larry isn't *at all* shy about expressing his opinions.

- When I asked Donna whether she was tired, she said, "Not *in the least*. I'm full of energy."

to look up: to locate information in a directory, dictionary, book, etc. **(S)**

- Elena suggested that we *look up* the store's telephone number on the Internet.

- Students should try to understand the meaning of a new word from context before *looking* the word *up* in the dictionary.

to wait on: to serve in a store or restaurant

- A very pleasant young clerk *waited on* me in that shop.

- The restaurant server asked us, "Has anyone *waited on* you yet?"

at least: a minimum of, no fewer (or less) than

- I spend *at least* two hours every night studying.

- Mike drinks *at least* a quart of water every day.

so far: until now, until the present time (also: **up to now, as of yet**)
This idiom is usually used with the present perfect tense.

- *So far*, this year has been excellent for business. I hope that the good luck continues.

- How many idioms have we studied in this book *up to now?*

- *As of yet*, we have not had an answer from him.

to take a walk, hike, etc.: to go for a walk, hike, etc.
A *hike* involves challenging, strenuous walking, usually up a hill or mountain.

- Last evening we *took a walk* around the park.

- Let's *take a hike* up Cowles Mountain this afternoon.

to take a trip: to go on a journey, to travel

- I'm so busy at work that I have no time to *take a trip*.

- During the summer holidays, the Thompsons *took a trip* to Europe.

to try on: to wear clothes to check the style or fit before buying **(S)**

- He *tried on* several suits before he picked out a blue one.

- Why don't you *try* these shoes *on* next?

to think over: to consider carefully before deciding **(S)**

- I'd like to *think over* your offer first. Then can we talk it over tomorrow?

- You don't have to give me your decision now. *Think* it *over* for a while.

to take place: to occur, to happen according to plan

- The regular meetings of the committee *take place* in Constitution Hall.

- I thought that the celebration was *taking place* at John's house.

to put away: to remove from sight, to put in the proper place **(S)**

- Please *put away* your papers before you open the test booklet.

- John *put* the notepad *away* in his desk when he was finished with it.

EXERCISES

Choose the appropriate idiomatic expression to substitute for the italicized word or words in each sentence below. Idioms from previous lessons are indicated by number.

1. You'll have *to locate* his number in the telephone book.
   a. to think over
   b. to wait on
   c. to look up

2. Let's *go on a challenging walk* in the mountains this weekend.
   a. take a hike
   b. take a trip
   c. take part in

3. You ought to spend *a minimum of* an hour outside in the fresh air.
   a. in the least
   b. as usual (Lesson 2)
   c. at least

4. Would you like me to help you *choose* a new dress for the dance?
   a. pick out (Lesson 3)
   b. try on
   c. put away

5. I've always wanted *to journey* to Alaska during the summer.
   a. to take a walk
   b. to take a trip
   c. to take a hike

6. It took a long time for the store clerk *to serve* us.
   a. to call on (Lesson 2)
   b. to take part in
   c. to wait on

7. I don't enjoy house cleaning *to any degree*.
   a. at all
   b. up to now
   c. at last (Lesson 2)

8. Our guest will arrive soon; please *remove* your dirty clothes *from sight*.
   a. try on
   b. put away
   c. get off (Lesson 1)

9. I'll *switch on* the light so that we can see better in here.
   a. be in on
   b. turn on (Lesson 1)
   c. try on

10. James didn't want *to be involved in* the preparations for the conference.
    a. to take part in
    b. to take place
    c. to try on

B *Fill in each blank with the appropriate form of an idiomatic expression from this lesson.*

MARA: Where's the store clerk?

KIM: I don't know. It's taking her too long to _____ us.

MARA: I don't like the service in this store _____. I feel like leaving right now.

KIM: Don't do that. How many dresses have you tried on _____?

MARA: Oh, I've tried on about eight dresses.

KIM: Well, after all that time and effort, you should buy _____ one, don't you think?

MARA: No, never mind. I'm so upset that I need to _____ outside in the fresh air.

KIM: Mara, I think that you're making the wrong decision. This is really a nice dress at a great price. You should _____ it _____.

MARA: Well . . . I guess a few more minutes of waiting won't make a difference.

Lesson 5

to look out: to be careful or cautious (also: **to watch out**)
Both of these idioms can occur with the preposition *for*.

- *"Look out!"* Jeffrey cried as his friend almost stepped in front of a car.

- *Look out for* reckless drivers whenever you cross the street.

- Small children should always *watch out for* strangers offering candy.

to shake hands: to exchange greetings by clasping hands

- When people meet for the first time, they usually *shake hands*.

- The student warmly *shook hands* with his old professor.

to get back: to return **(S)**

- Mr. Harris *got back* from his business trip to Chicago this morning.

- Could you *get* the children *back* home by five o'clock?

to catch a cold: to become sick with a cold of the nose or throat **(S)**

- If you go out in this rain, you will surely *catch a cold*.

- Every winter I *catch a* terrible *cold*.

to get over: to recover from an illness; to accept a loss or sorrow

- It took me over a month *to get over* my cold, but I'm finally well now.

- It seems that Mr. Mason will never *get over* the death of his wife.

to make up one's mind: to reach a decision, to decide finally

- Sally is considering several colleges to attend, but she hasn't *made up her mind* yet.

- When are you going to *make up your mind* about your vacation plans?

to change one's mind: to alter one's decision or opinion

- We have *changed our minds* and are going to Canada instead of California this summer.

- Matthew has *changed his mind* several times about buying a new car.

for the time being: temporarily (also: **for now**)

- *For the time being*, Janet is working as a waitress, but she really hopes to become an actress soon.

- We're living in an apartment *for now*, but soon we'll be looking for a house to buy.

for good: permanently, forever

- Ruth has returned to Canada *for good*. She won't ever live in the United States again.

- Are you finished with school *for good*, or will you continue your studies some day?

to call off: to cancel **(S)**

- The referee *called off* the soccer game because of the darkness.

- The president *called* the meeting *off* because she had to leave town.

to put off: to postpone **(S)**

- Many students *put off* doing their assignments until the last minute.

- Let's *put* the party *off* until next weekend, okay?

in a hurry: hurried, rushed (also: **in a rush**)

- Alex seems *in a hurry;* he must be late for his train again.

- She's always *in a rush* in the morning to get the kids to school.

EXERCISES

 Choose the appropriate idiomatic expression to substitute for the italicized word or words in each sentence below. Idioms from previous lessons are indicated by number.

A

1. Will you *return* in time for dinner or will you be home late tonight?
   a. put off
   b. get back
   c. take place (Lesson 4)

2. It took me a long time *to recover from* the sadness of losing my dog.
   a. to get over
   b. to look out
   c. to change my mind

3. After reading a lot of articles, she finally *discovered* some interesting facts about the case.
   a. got up
   b. turned on
   c. came up with

4. James has tried to quit smoking before, but this time he wants to quit *forever.*
   a. for the time being
   b. for good
   c. in a hurry

5. At the last moment, Judy *altered her decision* about getting married so quickly.

   a. changed her mind

   b. made up her mind

   c. never mind (Lesson 2)

6. Judy wanted *to postpone* the wedding for another two or three months.
   a. to call off

   b. to put off

   c. to turn off (Lesson 1)

7. I'd like you to *put* those toys *in the proper place* before they get broken.
   a. to put away (Lesson 4)

   b. to take out (Lesson 3)

   c. to look out

8. If you don't wear a sweater in this cold weather, you'll *become sick.*
   a. get over

   b. catch a cold

   c. tire out (Lesson 2)

9. I still have a lot of work to do, but I feel like stopping *temporarily.*
   a. in a hurry

   b. to shake hands

   c. for now

10. If you don't *be careful,* you'll cut your hands on that sharp knife.
    a. look up (Lesson 4)

    b. watch out

    c. make up your mind

B *Fill in each blank with the appropriate form of an idiomatic expression from this lesson.*

TODD: Mark! I was wondering when you would _____ home!

MARK: Sorry, Todd. I had a late meeting today. I left _____ to catch the bus home, but I missed it.

TODD: That's too bad. Hey, do you think I should go to a movie tonight with Sheila, or not? I can't _____.

MARK: What do you mean? You haven't _____ your cold yet, have you?

TODD: No, I haven't, but I feel much better.

MARK: I think that you only feel better _____ because you stayed home all day.

TODD: I guess you're right. Do you think that I should _____ going with her until another time?

MARK: That would be my advice.

Lesson 6

to hang out: to spend time, usually being idle or unproductive

- Luka likes to *hang out* and play video games with his friends.

- I spent all weekend *hanging out* at home. I didn't do anything exciting.

to hang up: to place clothes on a hook or hanger **(S)**; to replace the receiver on the phone at the end of a conversation **(S)**

- Would you like me to *hang up* your coat for you in the closet?

- The operator told me to *hang* the phone *up* and call the number again.

to count on: to trust someone in time of need (also: **to depend on**)

- I can *count on* my parents to help me in an emergency.

- Don't *depend on* Frank to lend you any money; he doesn't have any.

to make friends: to become friendly with others

- Patricia is a shy girl and doesn't *make friends* easily.

- During the cruise Ronald *made friends* with almost everyone on the ship.

out of order: not in working condition

- The elevator was *out of order,* so we had to walk to the tenth floor of the building.

- We couldn't use the soft drink machine because it was *out of order.*

to get to: to be able to do something special; to arrive at a place, such as home, work, etc.
For the second definition, do not use the preposition *to* with the words *home* or *there.*

- The children *got to* stay up late and watch a good movie for the family.

- I missed the bus and couldn't *get to* the office until ten o'clock.

- When are you planning to *get home* tonight?

to look over: to examine, to inspect closely (also: **to go over, to read over, to check over**) **(S)**
Go over is different from the other forms because it is not separable.

- I want to *look* my homework *over* again before I give it to the teacher.

- The politician *went over* his speech before the important presentation.

- You should never sign any legal paper without *checking* it *over* first.

to have (time) off: to have free time, not to have to work (also: **to take time off (S)**)
The related form **(S)** *to take time off* is used when someone makes a decision to have free time, usually to go on vacation or to relax.

- Every morning the company workers *have* time *off* for a coffee break.

- Several workers *took* the afternoon *off* to go to a baseball game.

to go on: to happen; to resume, to continue (also: **to keep on**)

- Many people gathered near the accident to see what was *going on*.

- The moderator tried to interrupt him, but he *went on* for another ten minutes.

- The speaker *kept on* talking even though most of the audience had left.

to put out: to extinguish **(S)**

- No smoking is allowed in here. Please *put out* your cigarette.

- The fire fighters worked hard to *put* the brush fire *out*.

all of a sudden: suddenly, without warning (also: **all at once**)

- *All of a sudden* Ed appeared at the door. We weren't expecting him to drop by.

- *All at once* Millie got up and left the house without any explanation.

ahead of time: before a scheduled time or event

- I knew *ahead of time* that Craig was coming to dinner, so I cooked extra food.

- If you take time off of work, you should tell your boss *ahead of time*.

EXERCISES

 Choose the appropriate idiomatic expression to substitute for the italicized word or words in each sentence below. Idioms from previous lessons are indicated by number.

1. The businessman *inspected* the contract *carefully* before signing it.
   a. looked over
   b. looked out (Lesson 5)
   c. counted on

2. What's *happening*, John? The smoke alarm is ringing but there's no fire!
   a. putting out
   b. going on
   c. hanging up

3. The dark clouds rolled in quickly and it began to rain *without warning*.
   a. all along (Lesson 2)
   b. out of order
   c. all of a sudden

Introduction

"Welcome. It is my pleasure to explain to you my findings on _____ ."

Process

"On this first slide, you will see _____ . This illustrates _____ .

"Now let me explain what we did for the paper cup activity"
    List procedure:

"Now let me explain what we did for the straw activity"
    List procedure:

"Here is a chart that demonstrates the Nicotine Withdrawal based upon the weeks of cessation of smoking. Take careful notice of the peak relapse, which takes place during the first two weeks. The severity of withdrawal symptoms can be seen at about four weeks time. Throughout the first ten weeks, you will see an increase in appetite and weight gain. This chart only displays thirteen weeks of time, but the craving for nicotine is quite apparent throughout that time.

Even though quitting initially will seem painful and unbearable, in the long-term you will be on your way to a healthier and happier you.

Q/A
Are there any questions about these findings?

Conclusion
I hope that you found some valuable information in my research. Thank you for allowing me to share this data with you today.

4. When do you think that we'll *arrive* at the hotel this evening?
   a. get on (Lesson 1)
   b. go on
   c. get to

5. I'm busy this week, but I hope to *have time free* next week.
   a. to take my time (Lesson 3)
   b. to have time off
   c. to check over

6. *Gradually* I'm learning how to play tennis, thanks to my patient instructor.
   a. Little by little (Lesson 2)
   b. All at once
   c. In a hurry (Lesson 5)

7. It's nice to know that I can *trust* you to help me when I need it.
   a. count on
   b. look over
   c. make friends

8. The phone is making noise because you forgot *to replace* the receiver.
   a. to go over
   b. to take place (Lesson 4)
   c. to hang up

9. After school, Ben likes to *spend time* with his girlfriend.
   a. go on
   b. hang out
   c. hang up

10. The students were happy because they *were able to* leave class early.

  a. took time off to

  b. went on

  c. got to

B *Fill in each blank with the appropriate form of an idiomatic expression from this lesson.*

TINA: Hi, Jessica, it's Tina. I've got great news!

JESSICA: _____, tell me what it is.

TINA: Well, I _____ some extra _____ from work, so I'm going to a beach resort next week. Do you want to come?

JESSICA: I'd love to, but I can't go on vacation _____ like that. I have to tell my boss ahead of time.

TINA: That's too bad. It would have been fun to _____ together in the sun.

JESSICA: Yeah, but I'm sure you will _____ with all the other people there.

TINA: I sure hope so. Well, I have to _____ now. I've got to start packing for my trip. Good bye!

Lesson 7

to point out: to show, to indicate, to bring to one's attention **(S)**

- What important buildings did the tour guide *point out* to you?

- The teacher *pointed out* the mistakes in my composition.

- A friend *pointed* the famous actor *out* to me.

to be up: to expire, to be finished
This idiom is used only with the word *time* as the subject.

- "The time *is up,*" the teacher said at the end of the test period.

- We have to leave the tennis court because our hour *is up*; some other people want to use it now.

to be over: to be finished, to end (also: **to be through**)
This idiom is used for activities and events.

- After the dance *was over,* we all went to a restaurant.

- The meeting *was through* ten minutes earlier than everyone expected.

on time: exactly at the correct time, punctually

- I thought that Margaret would arrive late, but she was right *on time*.

- Did you get to work *on time* this morning, or did rush hour traffic delay you?

in time to: before the time necessary to do something

- We entered the theater just *in time* to see the beginning of the movie.

- The truck was not able to stop *in time* to prevent an accident.

to get better, worse, etc.: to become better, worse, etc.
This idiom is often used with adjectives such as *any* and *much*.

- Heather has been sick for a month, but now she is *getting better.*

- I hope the economy doesn't *get* any *worse* than it is now.

to get sick, well, tired, busy, wet, etc.: to become sick, well, tired, busy, wet, etc.
This idiom consists of a combination of *get* and various adjectives.

- Ilhan *got sick* last week and has been in bed since that time.

- Every afternoon I *get* very *hungry,* so I eat a snack.

had better: should, ought to, be advisable to
This idiom is most often used in contracted form *(I'd better).*

- I think *you'd better* speak to Mr. White right away about this matter.

- The doctor told the patient that *he'd better* go home and rest.

would rather: prefer to (also: **would just as soon**)

- *Would* you *rather* have the appointment this Friday or next Monday?

- I *would just as soon* go for a walk as watch TV right now.

to call it a day/night: to stop working for the rest of the day/night

- Ian tried to repair his car engine all morning before he *called it a day* and went fishing.

- We've been working hard on this project all evening; let's *call it a night.*

to figure out: to solve, to find a solution **(S)**; to understand **(S)**

- How long did it take you *to figure out* the answer to the math problem?

- I was never able to *figure it out.*

to think of: to have a (good or bad) opinion of

This idiom is often used in the negative or with adjectives such as *much* and *highly.*

- I don't *think* much *of* him as a baseball player; he's a slow runner and a poor hitter.

- James *thinks* highly *of* his new boss, who is a kind and helpful person.

EXERCISES

 A *Choose the appropriate idiomatic expression to substitute for the italicized word or words in each sentence below. Idioms from previous lessons are indicated by number.*

1. We *were able to* visit the zoo when the animals were very active.
   a. would rather
   b. had better
   c. got to (Lesson 6)

2. All of this work in the garden has tired me out; let's *stop working.*
   a. be over
   b. call it a day
   c. be up

3. I can't *understand* Professor Jones at all; he's a very good teacher, but sometimes he says foolish things.
   a. figure out
   b. make up my mind about (Lesson 5)
   c. point out

4. I *prefer to* eat in tonight than to eat out; what do you think?
   a. would rather
   b. had better
   c. so far (Lesson 4)

5. The police officer put a parking ticket on the car because the time on the meter *had expired*.

   a. was over

   b. was not on time

   c. was up

6. I don't *have a good opinion of* our new neighbors; they're not very friendly.

   a. make friends with (Lesson 6)

   b. get better with

   c. think much of

7. This problem is too difficult for me *to solve* by myself.

   a. to point out

   b. to be over

   c. to figure out

8. We were late to the party, but we got there *before the time* to eat dinner.

   a. to wait on

   b. in time to

   c. on time

9. Jan couldn't wait for the meeting *to end* so that she could go home.

   a. to call off (Lesson 5)

   b. to be through

   c. to get worse

10. It was supposed to be a surprise, but Larry knew about the birthday party *from the beginning*.

    a. all along (Lesson 2)

    b. on time

    c. to call it a night

B *Fill in each blank with the appropriate form of an idiomatic expression from this lesson.*

JAKE: If you're going to take classes this semester, you

        _____ register soon.

KIRSTEN: I know, but I can't make up my mind which classes to take. I

        need science credits, but I _____ take more art

        classes.

JAKE: I can't _____ why you like art classes so much.

        They won't help you get a job, you know.

KIRSTEN: Must I _____ again to you that my dad is a

        professional artist?

JAKE: I know, but I still don't _____ much

        _____ art as a career. It's not secure enough.

        You should definitely take the science classes.

KIRSTEN: Maybe I will. Then at least I'd complete my class requirements

        _____ graduate this semester.

Lesson 8

to be about to: to be at the moment of doing something, to be ready
This idiom is often used with the adverb *just*.

- I was *about to* leave when you called me.

- Oh, hi, John. We're *just about to* eat dinner.

to turn around: to move or face in the opposite direction **(S)**; to completely change the condition of **(S)**

- She *turned around* to wave goodbye before getting on the airplane.

- The man *turned* his car *around* and drove back the way he came.

- The company has been very successful since the new business manager was able to *turn* it *around*.

to take turns: to alternate, to change people while doing something

- During the trip, Darlene and I *took turns* driving so that neither of us would tire out.

- I have to make sure that my two sons *take turns* playing the video game.

to pay attention (to): to look at and listen to someone while they are speaking, to concentrate

- Please *pay attention* to me while I'm speaking to you!

- You'll have to *pay* more *attention* in class if you want to get a good grade.

to brush up on: to review something in order to refresh one's memory

- Before I travelled to Mexico, I *brushed up on* my Spanish; I haven't practiced it since high school.

- In order to take that advance math class, Sidney will have to *brush up on* his algebra.

over and over (again): repeatedly (also: **time after time, time and again**)

- The actress studied her lines *over and over* until she knew them well.

- Children have difficulty remembering rules, so it's often necessary to repeat them *over and over again.*

- *Time and again* I have to remind Arturo to put on his seatbelt in the car.

to wear out: to use something until it has no value or worth anymore, to make useless through wear **(S)**

- When I *wear out* these shoes, I'll have to buy some that last longer.

- What do you do with your clothes after you *wear* them *out?*

to throw away: to discard, to dispose of **(S)**

- I generally *throw away* my clothes when I wear them out.

- Don't *throw* the magazines *away;* I haven't read them yet.

to fall in love: to begin to love
This idiom is used with the expression *at first sight* to indicate a sudden love for someone not known well.

- Ben and Sal *fell in love* in high school, and got married after graduation.

- Have you ever *fallen in love at first sight?*

to go out (with): to go on a date (with); to date repeatedly

- Andre and I are *going out* on Saturday. We are going to have dinner at my favorite restaurant.

- Eda *went out with* Rick for six months, but now she is *going out with* someone else.

to go out: to stop functioning; to stop burning; to leave home or work (also: **to step out**)

- The lights *went out* all over the city because of an electrical problem.

The campers didn't have to put out the fire because it *went out* by itself.

Gary isn't here right now; he *went out* to the store for a moment.

I have to *step out* of the office briefly to pick up a newspaper.

to break up (with): to stop dating

Leo and Heidi just *broke up* after dating for three years.

Tai *broke up with* his girlfriend because he fell in love with someone else.

EXERCISES

 Choose the appropriate idiomatic expression to substitute for the italicized word or words in each sentence below. Idioms from previous lessons are indicated by number.

1. Don't *discard* those old cardboard boxes; Jim can use them for packing his things when he moves to a new apartment.
   a. put away (Lesson 4)
   b. throw away
   c. wear out

2. If you had *concentrated on* what I said, I wouldn't have to repeat myself.
   a. paid attention to
   b. brushed up on
   c. turned around

3. I plan to stay in school *temporarily* and take more classes.
   a. at last (Lesson 2)
   b. over and over again
   c. for the time being (Lesson 5)

4. I think Karen and Greg would get along if they *went on a date* sometime.

    a. took turns

    b. went out

    c. wore out

5. Before George takes a college-level biology class, he should *review* his biology from high school.

    a. brush up on

    b. pay attention to

    c. be about to

6. I liked that movie so much that I could watch it *repeatedly.*

    a. right away (Lesson 1)

    b. taking turns

    c. over and over again

7. Betty can't *understand* why she's having trouble with her new DVD player.

    a. turn around

    b. figure out (Lesson 7)

    c. step out

8. Megan has been depressed ever since Troy *stopped dating* her.

    a. fell in love with

    b. paid attention to

    c. broke up with

9. Sally *was ready to* take a shower when the phone rang, so she didn't answered it.

    a. was about to

    b. took turns to

    c. had better (Lesson 7)

10. I'm tired of working; let's *leave home* for a while and shop for groceries.

   a. turn around

   b. go out

   c. call it a day (Lesson 7)

B *Fill in each blank with the appropriate form of an idiomatic expression from this lesson.*

LEE: Jan, you've _____ these shoes completely. Why do you keep them?

JAN: Don't ask me again, Lee! I've told you _____ they are my favorite pair.

LEE: I know, I know. Every time we _____ somewhere, you wear them.

JAN: It's terrible, isn't it? I know that I should _____ them _____, but they're so comfortable, I can't!

LEE: What if I said that I would buy a new pair for you—would you discard them then?

JAN: That's completely _____! This situation doesn't _____ money; it's about my feeling for the shoes.

LEE: Feeling for the shoes! Is it possible that you have _____ with them?

JAN: Yes, I guess I love them more than I love you!

Lesson 9

to wake up: to arise from sleep, to awaken **(S)**
Compare *wake up* and *get up* (Lesson 1) as used in the first example.

- Maggie *woke up* this morning very early, but she did not get up until about ten o'clock.

- My alarm clock *wakes* me *up* at the same time every day.

to be in charge of: to manage, to have responsibility for

- Jane *is in charge of* the office while Mrs. Haig is on a business trip.

- Who *is in charge of* arrangements for the dance next week?

as soon as: just after, when

- *As soon as* it started to snow, the children ran outside with big smiles on their faces.

- I'm busy now, but I'll meet you *as soon as* I've finished this work.

to have a good time: to enjoy oneself

- We all *had a good time* at the class reunion last night.

- Did you *have a good time* at the park? I really enjoyed it.

in no time: very quickly, rapidly
This idiom can be used with the idiom *at all* to add emphasis to the certainty of the statement.

- Mac said that he'd be ready to leave *in no time*.

- We thought that the meeting would take two hours, but it was over *in no time at all*.

to cut down on: to reduce, to lessen (also: **to cut back on**)

- In order to lose weight, you have *to cut down on* your intake of sugar.

- The doctor told me *to cut back on* exercise until my back injury heals.

to crack down on: to enforce or punish strictly

- The school has started to *crack down on* smoking. Students who smoke on campus will be suspended.

- Maura is finally *cracking down on* her son and making him help with the housework.

quite a few: many

- *Quite a few* students were absent yesterday; in fact, more than half of them were not there.

- We did not expect many people to attend the affair, but *quite a few* of our friends actually came.

used to: formerly did, had the habit of
This idiom is used to indicate a post situation, action, or habit that does not exist in the present. The idiom is always followed by a simple verb form.

- I *used to* live in New York, but I moved to California two years ago.

- Kim *used to* smoke cigarettes, but she stopped the habit last month.

to be used to: be accustomed to
This idiom refers to a situation, action, or habit that continues in the present. The idiom is always followed by a noun or gerund phrase.

- He *is used to* this climate now, so the changes in temperature do not affect him much.

- I *am used to* studying in the library, so it's difficult for me to study at home now.

to get used to: to become used to, to become adjusted to
This idiom describes the process of change that allows someone to be used to a situation, action, or habit.

- It took Yoshiko a long time *to get used to* the food that her American host family served her.

- Mark can't seem *to get used to* wearing contact lenses; recently he's been wearing his glasses a lot.

back and forth: in a backward and forward motion

- The restless lion kept pacing *back and forth* along the front of its cage.

- Grandmother finds it relaxing to sit in her rocking chair and move *back and forth*.

EXERCISES

 Choose the appropriate idiomatic expression to substitute for the italicized word or words in each sentence below. Idioms from previous lessons are indicated by number.

1. When we finally decided to eat out, we got ready *rapidly*.
   a. in no time
   b. on time (Lesson 7)
   c. as soon as

2. Joe has never been able *to become adjusted to* getting up early in the morning.
   a. used to
   b. to be used to
   c. to get used to

3. I have a lot of trouble breathing well when I run, so I guess that I should *reduce* smoking.

   a. be in charge of

   b. throw away (Lesson 8)

   c. cut down on

4. While I was reading in bed last night, the phone in the kitchen rang, so I had *to arise* to answer it.

   a. to wake up

   b. to get up (Lesson 1)

   c. to be used to

5. *Many* people at the beach were wearing jackets because the wind was cool.

   a. Quite a few

   b. As soon as

   c. Few and far between (Lesson 6)

6. The police are *strictly punishing* speeding in our neighborhood; I've already received two tickets this month.

   a. cracking down on

   b. having a good time

   c. getting used to

7. *When* my parents were ready to leave, we went out to dinner.

   a. At first (Lesson 1)

   b. As soon as

   c. All of a sudden (Lesson 6)

8. Jack *made* the engine of his car *useless* by forgetting to add oil to it regularly.

   a. got worse (Lesson 7)

   b. used to

   c. wore out (Lesson 8)

9. The boat was moving *in backward and forward motion* because of the large waves on the ocean.

   a. at least (Lesson 4)

   b. back and forth

   c. on purpose (Lesson 3)

10. Vera *had the habit* of biting her nails until they were very short, but now she's stopped doing that.

    a. has been used to

    b. used to

    c. cut back on

B *Fill in each blank with the appropriate form of an idiomatic expression from this lesson.*

ABE: Zeke! It's already 8 A.M. It's time for you to

_____.

ZEKE: What do you mean? It's the weekend, and I

_____ sleeping until at least 10 A.M. on

Saturdays!

ABE: Don't you remember? We're organizing a beach picnic for our

sports club today.

ZEKE: Oh, I forgot about that. Just give me fifteen more minutes. I can

be ready _____.

ABE: Look, there are things _____ to take to the beach

and to set up, like the volleyball net. We need to do it together.

ZEKE: Boy, why did you agree that we would _____ the

picnic? It's too much responsibility.

ABE: I didn't agree. You did!

ZEKE: Well, now I realize that I _____ going to these activities, but I have a lot less fun planning them!

Lesson 10

to make sure: to be sure, to ascertain (also: **to make certain**)

- Please *make sure* that you turn off the radio before you go out.

- Could you *make certain* of the time? I don't want to miss that TV show.

now and then: occasionally, sometimes (also: **from time to time, once in a while**)
Both *now and then* and *once in a while* can be preceded by the adjective *every*.
Another idiom with the same meaning and form is *every so often*.

- I don't see him very often, but *(every) now and then* we arrange to have lunch together.

- Gary gets a cold *(every) once in a while* even though he takes good care of himself.

- *Every so often* my brother and I get together for a camping trip.

- I like to sleep late in the morning *from time to time*.

to get rid of: to eliminate, to remove; to discard, to throw away

- Jerry tried hard to *get rid of* the stain on his shirt, but he never succeeded.

- The stain was so bad that Jerry finally had to *get rid of* his shirt.

every other (one): every second (one), alternate (ones)

- I play tennis with my father *every other* Saturday, so I usually play twice a month.

- There were twenty problems in the exercise, but the teacher told us only to do *every other* one. Actually, doing ten problems was difficult enough.

to go with: to match, to compare well in color or design often used with this idiom. (also: **to go together**)
Adverbs such as *well* and *poorly* are often used with this idiom.

- That striped shirt *goes* well *with* the gray pants, but the pants *go* poorly *with* those leather shoes.

- Both of those paintings are nice, but they don't *go together* at *all*.

first-rate: excellent, superb

- The food served in that four-star restaurant is truly *first-rate*.

- The Beverly Hills Hotel provides *first-rate* service to its guests.

to come from: to originate from
This idiom is commonly used in discussions of one's hometown, state, or country.

- What country in South America does she *come from?* She *comes from* Peru.

- I just learned that he really *comes from* Florida, not Texas.

- Where did this package *come from?* It was just sitting on our doorstep.

to make good time: to travel a sufficient distance at a reasonable speed
The adjective *excellent* can also be used.

- It rained during our entire hike up Mt. Hood, so we didn't *make good time*.

- We *made excellent time* on our trip to Florida; it only took five hours to drive there.

to mix up: to stir or shake well **(S)**; to confuse, to bewilder **(S)**
For the second definition, the passive forms *to be mixed up* or *to get mixed up* are often used.

- You should *mix up* the ingredients well before you put them in the pan.

- The teacher's poor explanation really *mixed* the students *up*.

- The students think it's their fault that they *are mixed up* so often.

to see about: to give attention or time to (also: **to attend to, to see to**)

- Who is going to *see about* getting us a larger room for the meeting?

- I'll *see to* arranging music for the wedding if you *attend* to the entertainment.

to make an impression: to influence another person's opinion of oneself (also: **to leave an impression**) **(S)**
This idiom is usually separated by an adjective such as *good* or *bad*.

- Abigail *made a* good *impression* during her job interview, so they offered her the position.

- With his awful manners and personality, Karsten *leaves a* bad *impression* on everyone he meets.

by heart: by memorizing

- He knows many passages from Shakespeare *by heart*.

- Do you know all the idioms you have studied in this book *by heart?*

EXERCISES

 Choose the appropriate idiomatic expression to substitute for the italicized word or words in each sentence below. Idioms from previous lessons are indicated by number.

1. Doug has such a strong personality, *he influences others' opinions of himself* wherever he goes.

   a. makes good time

   b. makes an impression

   c. has a good time (Lesson 9)

2. The manager wanted her assistant *to ascertain* when the products would be delivered.

   a. to make good time

   b. to get rid of

   c. to make sure

3. You should *stir* the milk and eggs before you add the butter.

   a. cut down on (Lesson 9)

   b. mix up

   c. come from

4. I was so nervous about giving the speech that I learned every word *by memorizing.*

   a. by myself (Lesson 3)

   b. by heart

   c. now and then

5. The weather is so bad today that we should definitely *postpone* the picnic.

   a. put off (Lesson 5)

   b. call off (Lesson 5)

   c. see about

6. Where does Jacek *originate from?* He has such an interesting accent.

   a. go with

   b. come from

   c. look over (Lesson 6)

7. The test instructions were so poorly written that the students *were confused* about what to do.

   a. were attended to

   b. paid attention (Lesson 8)

   c. were mixed up

8. This yellow tie doesn't *match* your blue jacket at all.

   a. go with

   b. get rid of

   c. come from

9. John enjoys going hiking with his friends. They take a hike together *every second* weekend.

   a. every now and then

   b. every other

   c. all weekend long (Lesson 3)

10. This tablecloth is too old to use anymore; would you mind if we *discard* it?

    a. get rid of

    b. come from

    c. see to

B *Fill in each blank with the appropriate form of an idiomatic expression from this lesson.*

JOANNE: Do you want this shirt, Helene? It doesn't fit me, so I'm going to _____ it.

HELENE: Sure, I'll take it. It will _____ the pants I'm going to wear to my audition tomorrow.

JOANNE: Where is your audition?

HELENE: At the Grand Street Theater downtown. There's a lot of traffic in that area, but if I take the subway I can _____.

JOANNE: That's a _____ theater. Its shows always get great reviews.

HELENE: I know. I really hope that I _____ good

_____. I've already memorized the role

_____ so I won't make a mistake.

JOANNE: I'm sure you'll do well. Just _____ that you're

not late getting there!

Lesson 11

to keep out: not to enter, not allow to enter **(S)**

- There was a large sign outside the door that said, "Danger! *Keep out!*"

- I've told you to *keep* the dog *out* of the house.

to keep away (from): to stay at a distance (from) **(S)**; to avoid use of (also: **stay away from**)

- Please be sure to *keep* the children *away from* the street!

- The signs on the burned-out house said, "*Keep Away!* Danger Zone."

- It's important to *stay away from* dangerous drugs.

to find fault with: to criticize, to complain about something

- It is very easy *to find fault with* the work of others, but more difficult to accept criticism of one's own work.

- Mrs. Johnson is always *finding fault with* her children, though they really try to please her.

to be up to: to be dependent on the decision of another; to be doing as a regular activity; to feel able to do something
The second definition is most often used in a question as a form of greeting.

- I don't care whether we go to the reception or not. It's *up to* you.

- Hi, Evan. I haven't seen you in a while. What have you *been up to?*

- Alexi *isn't up to* going on a hike; his broken foot is still holding.

ill at ease: uncomfortable or worried in a situation

- Speaking in front of a large audience makes many people feel *ill at ease*.

- My wife and I were *ill at ease* because our daughter was late coming home from a date.

to do over: to revise, to do again **(S)**
A noun or pronoun must separate the two parts of this idiom.

- You'd better *do* the letter *over* because it is written so poorly.

- José made so many mistakes in his homework that the teacher made him *do* it *over*.

to look into: to investigate, to examine carefully (also: **to check into**)

- The police *are looking into* the matter of the stolen computers.

- The congressional committee will *check into* the financial dealings of the government contractor.

to take hold of: to grasp, to grip with the hands

- You should *take hold of* the railing as you go down those steep stairs.

- The blind man *took hold of* my arm as I led him across the street.

to get through: to finish, to complete
This idiom is followed either by the *-ing* form of a verb (a gerund) or by the preposition *with*.

- I didn't *get through* studying last night until almost eleven o'clock.

- At what time does your wife *get through with* work every day?

from now on: from this time into the future

- Mr. Lee's doctor told him to cut down on eating fatty foods *from now on*, or else he might suffer heart disease.

● I'm sorry that I dropped by at a bad time. *From now on* I'll call ahead of time.

to keep track of: to keep or maintain a record of; to remember the location or status of

● Steve *keeps track of* all the long-distance telephone calls related to his business that he makes from his home or cell phone.

● With seven small children, how do the Wilsons *keep track of* all of them?

to get carried away: to act in an extreme manner
A related idiom is **to go overboard**.

● Even if you have an awful day at work, you shouldn't *get carried away* and quit your job.

● James *went overboard* while shopping for his wife's birthday present. He spent way too much money!

EXERCISES

 A *Choose the appropriate idiomatic expression to substitute for the italicized word or words in each sentence below. Idioms from previous lessons are indicated by number.*

1. It's difficult for old people *to remember the location of* personal possessions such as keys.

   a. to keep track of

   b. to keep away from

   c. to take hold of

2. I haven't seen Jasmine in a long time. I wonder what she *has been doing.*

   a. has gotten through

   b. has to do with (Lesson 8)

   c. has been up to

3. Jeff agreed *to give attention to* organizing the beach barbecue this weekend.

    a. to find fault with

    b. to see about (Lesson 10)

    c. to do over

4. The unfriendly man told the neighborhood boys, "I don't want any of you coming in my yard. *Don' t enter!"*

    a. Keep out!

    b. Get carried away!

    c. Put out! (Lesson 6)

5. Vivian felt *uncomfortable* at the party because she didn't know anyone there; they were all complete strangers to her.

    a. mixed up (Lesson 10)

    b. ill at ease

    c. all right (Lesson 2)

6. To open the door, you have *to grasp* it firmly and pull hard.

    a. to take hold of

    b. to get through

    c. to find fault with

7. *Until now* I haven't broken any bones in my body.

    a. At last (Lesson 2)

    b. From now on

    c. So far (Lesson 4)

8. Lita made so many mistakes in her essay that the teacher told her *to revise it*.

    a. to find fault with it

    b. to do it over

    c. to check into it

9. I acted in an *extreme manner* when my friends surprised me with a big birthday celebration—I was screaming and jumping around with joy.

   a. got carried away

   b. kept out

   c. was ill at ease

10. Mr. Smith asked the police *to investigate* the theft of his car radio last week.

    a. to look for (Lesson 2)

    b. to look over (Lesson 6)

    c. to look into

B *Fill in each blank with the appropriate form of an idiomatic expression from this lesson.*

MAX: Jeff, are you still busy?

JEFF: Of course I am! Didn't you see the sign on my door. It says,

"_____!"

MAX: Sorry, Jeff. I just wanted to know when you're going to

_____ with your work.

JEFF: I need at least another five hours. The professor found so many

mistakes in my research paper that I have to

_____ it _____.

MAX: Oh, I didn't realize that.

JEFF: I know one thing—I'm going to start all my work much earlier

and do it more carefully _____.

MAX: That's a good idea. Say, would you like to watch TV and relax

for a minute?

JEFF: Are you kidding? I have to _____ TV if I'm going to finish this work.

MAX: Well, it's you. I can write more easily after I take a short break. Would you like me to read what you've done so far?

JEFF: No way. I know what will happen—you'll just _____ it.

MAX: Okay, then. I'll just go away and leave you alone.

JEFF: Thanks, Max. Sorry I'm acting so strange. I'm just feeling _____ about this paper. I need to get it done by tomorrow.

MAX: I understand. Just don't _____ and be angry at your friends!

Lesson 12

up to date: modern; current, timely
Hyphens (-) separate the parts of this idiom when it precedes a noun form, as in the third example. The verb *to update* derives from this idiom.

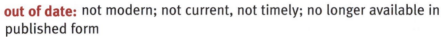

- The president insisted that the company bring its aging equipment *up to date*.

- This catalog is not *up to date*. It was published several years ago.

- The news program gave an *up-to-date* account of the nuclear accident. The newscaster said that he would update the news report every half hour.

out of date: not modern; not current, not timely; no longer available in published form
Again, hyphens separate the parts of this idiom when it precedes a noun form as, in the second example. The passive verb *to be outdated* derives from this idiom.

- Many people buy new cars when their old cars become *out of date*.

- I don't know why Gene likes to wear *out-of-date* clothing. His clothes are so outdated that even his girlfriend hates to be seen with him.

- This book can't be ordered any more because it is *out of date*.

to blow up: to inflate, to fill with air **(S)**; to explode, to destroy (or be destroyed) by explosion **(S)**

- Daddy, could you please *blow up* this balloon for me?

- When the airplane crashed into the ground, it *blew up* immediately.

- The military had to *blow* the missile *up* in midair when it started to go the wrong way.

to catch fire: to begin to burn

- ● Don't stand too close to the gas stove. Your clothes may *catch fire.*

- ● No one seems to know how the old building *caught fire.*

to burn down: to destroy completely by fire; to burn slowly, but completely (usually said of candles) **(S)**

- ● The fire spread so quickly that the firefighters could not prevent the whole block of buildings from *burning down.*

- ● There was a large amount of wax on the table where the candles had *burned down.*

to burn up: to destroy completely by fire **(S)**; to make angry or very annoyed **(S)** (also: **to tick off**)
To burn up and *to burn down* (previous idiom) share the first definition but also have different definitions.

- ● She didn't want anyone to see the letter, so she *burned* it *up* and threw the ashes away.

- ● It really *burns* me *up* that he borrowed my car without asking me first.

- ● Mike got *ticked off* that his friends never offered to help him move to his new apartment. He had to do everything himself.

to burn out: to stop functioning because of overuse; to make tired from too much work **(S)**

- ● This light bulb has *burned out.* Could you get another one?

- ● Studying all day for my final exams has really *burned* me *out.*

stands to reason: to be clear and logical

This idiom is almost always used with the pronoun subject *it* and is followed by a *that* clause.

- *It stands to reason that* a person without experience cannot do the work as well as an experienced one.

- *It stands to reason that* he isn't going to pass the course if he never studies.

to break out: to become widespread suddenly

- An epidemic of measles *broke out* in Chicago this past week.

- If a nuclear war ever *breaks out,* it is unlikely that many people will survive.

- The news says that a large fire has *broken out* in a huge chemical plant.

as for: regarding, concerning (also: **as to**)

- *As for* the money, we will simply have to borrow some more from the bank.

- There is no doubt *as to* her intelligence; she's the smartest one in the class.

for one thing: for example, for instance

This idiom is used when giving a detail to support a statement or opinion.

- My dog is my best friend. *For one thing,* he is always there when I need him.

- Why don't you like your new roommate?
  Because she's very messy, *for one thing.* She leaves her things all over our apartment.

to feel sorry for: to pity, to feel compassion for (also: **to take pity on**)

- Don't you *feel sorry for* someone who has to work the night shift?

- I helped drive Pierre around when he broke his foot because I *took pity on* him.

EXERCISES

Choose the appropriate idiomatic expression to substitute for the italicized word or words in each sentence below. Idioms from previous lessons are indicated by number.

1. I had to use a lot of paper and matches before I was able to get the wood in the fireplace *to begin to burn*.
   a. to burn down
   b. to catch fire
   c. to burn up

2. If you stay up late every night, it *seems logical* that you'll tire yourself out.
   a. stands to reason
   b. goes with (Lesson 10)
   c. feels sorry for

3. The coach *inflated* several of the players' soccer balls that were too soft.
   a. broke out
   b. got rid of (Lesson 10)
   c. blew up

4. *From the beginning* I knew that I wanted to go to medical school and to become a doctor.
   a. All along (Lesson 2)
   b. As for
   c. For one thing

5. This set of reference books is so old that the library should buy one that is more *current*.
   a. out of date
   b. first-rate (Lesson 10)
   c. up to date

6. I *pity* Marilyn because everything of value in her house was stolen by thieves.

   a. tick off

   b. count on (Lesson 6)

   c. feel sorry for

7. If you continue without taking a break, this difficult work will *make you tired*.

   a. burn you out

   b. burn you up

   c. burn you down

8. Those two sisters look so much alike that I often get *confused* about their names.

   a. mixed up (Lesson 10)

   b. broken out

   c. out of date

9. *Regarding* me, I don't care where we go today. It's up to you.

   a. To be about to (Lesson 8)

   b. As for

   c. To think of (Lesson 7)

10. It *makes me annoyed* that Jocelyn didn't call to cancel our appointment.

    a. burns me up

    b. breaks me out

    c. burns me down

B *Fill in each blank with the appropriate form of an idiomatic expression from this lesson.*

MATT: Have you heard the news? A big fire _____ in the downtown area early this morning. A whole block was affected.

LISA: Really? How many buildings have _____?

MATT: More than ten, I believe. Haven't you seen the smoke in the air?

LISA: Yes, I wondered what that was. Why doesn't the fire department have the fire under control by now?

MATT: Well, their equipment is so _____ that it doesn't work well.

LISA: Boy, I bet that the people who lost their stores are really _____ about that. I would be very angry if it was my business.

MATT: _____ me, I _____ all the workers who have lost their jobs because of the fire.

LISA: It _____ that the city government is going to have to buy _____ equipment now.

MATT: Let's hope so.

Lesson 13

to break down: to stop functioning

Compare this idiom with *to burn out* in Lesson 12. *To burn out* means that electrical equipment becomes hot from overuse and stops functioning. *To break down* means that something stops functioning mechanically, whether from overuse or not.

- I just bought my new car yesterday and already it has *broken down*.

- The elevator *broke down*, so we walked all the way up to the top floor.

to turn out: to become or result; to appear, to attend (also: **to come out**)

The noun form **turnout** derives from the second definition of the idiom.

- Most parents wonder how their children will *turn out* as adults.

- Hundreds of people *came out* for the demonstration against new taxes.

- What was the *turnout* for the public hearing on the education reforms?

once in a blue moon: rarely, infrequently

- Snow falls on the city of San Diego, California, *once in a blue moon*.

- *Once in a blue moon* my wife and I eat at a very expensive restaurant.

to give up: to stop trying; to stop a bad habit **(S)**; to surrender **(S)**

- I'm sure that you can accomplish this task. Don't *give up* yet!

- If you *give up* smoking now, you will probably live a longer life.

- The soldiers *gave* themselves *up* in the face of stronger enemy forces.

to cross out: to cancel by marking with a horizontal line **(S)**

- The teacher *crossed out* several incorrect words in Tanya's composition.

- I *crossed* the last line *out* of my letter because it had the wrong tone to it.

to take for granted: not to appreciate fully **(S)**; to assume to be true without giving much thought **(S)**
A noun or pronoun often follows the verb *take*.

- Bruno *took* his wife *for granted* until once when he was very sick and needed her constant attention for a week.

- He spoke English so well that I *took* it *for granted* he was an American.

- He *took for granted* that I wasn't American because I spoke English so poorly!

to take into account: to consider a fact while evaluating a situation **(S)**
A noun or pronoun often follows the verb *take*.

- The judge *took* the prisoner's young age *into account* before sentencing him to three months in jail.

- Educators should *take into account* the cultural backgrounds of students when planning a school curriculum.

to make clear: to clarify, to explain **(S)**

- Please *make* it *clear* to Josef that he should never act so impolitely again.

- The supervisor *made* it *clear* to the workers that they had to increase their productivity.

clear cut: clearly stated, definite, apparent

- The president's message was *clear cut:* The company had to reduce personnel immediately.

- Professor Larsen is well known for his interesting and *clear-cut* presentations.

to have on: to be wearing **(S)**

- How do you like the hat that Grace *has on* today?

- When Sally came into the room, I *had* nothing *on* except my shorts.

to come to: to regain consciousness; to equal, to amount to

- At first they thought that the man was dead, but soon he *came to.*

- The bill for groceries at the supermarket *came to* fifty dollars.

to call for: to require; to request, to urge

- This cake recipe *calls for* some baking soda, but we don't have any.

- The members of Congress *called for* new laws to regulate the banking industry.

EXERCISES

 A *Choose the appropriate idiomatic expression to substitute for the italicized word or words in each sentence below. Idioms from previous lessons are indicated by number.*

1. The majority of the investors at the shareholders' meeting *urged* the resignation of the chairman of the board.
   a. called for
   b. took for granted
   c. are looking into (Lesson 11)

2. How many people *appeared* for the baseball game yesterday?
   a. turned out
   b. came to
   c. turned around (Lesson 8)

3. My reason for voting "no" is very *apparent:* I disagree completely with the position of other committee members on this matter.
   a. once in a blue moon
   b. clear cut
   c. made clear

4. There was a big traffic jam on the freeway when a truck *stopped functioning* in one of the middle lanes.

   a. burned down (Lesson 12)

   b. gave up

   c. broke down

5. Mrs. Thomas was very surprised when she received the bill for her hospital stay. It *equalled* almost ten thousand dollars.

   a. crossed out

   b. came from (Lesson 10)

   c. came to

6. Aaron *had the habit to* eat a lot of sweets until he decided to lose weight.

   a. is used to (Lesson 9)

   b. gave up

   c. used to (Lesson 9)

7. That's a very nice dress that you *are wearing*. Where did you buy it?

   a. have on

   b. take into account

   c. take for granted

8. As it *resulted,* I didn't have to worry about the game; we won it easily.

   a. turned out

   b. made clear

   c. was over (Lesson 7)

9. The gang of criminals *surrendered* to the police after eight hours of hiding in the warehouse.

   a. crossed out

   b. gave up

   c. looked out (Lesson 5)

10. Joe's mother *considered the fact* that Joe was trying to help his brother when the accident took place.

    a. took for granted

    b. made clear

    c. took into account

B *Fill in each blank with the appropriate form of an idiomatic expression from this lesson.*

MRS. LEE: Hello. How are you?

CASHIER: Fine, ma'am. Only buying a few groceries today, I see.

MRS. LEE: Yes. As it _____, I only have a few dollars with me.

CASHIER: That shirt you _____ really goes nicely with your eyes.

MRS. LEE: Thank you. I just bought it this morning.

CASHIER: Oh, no! The cash register just _____. None of the buttons are working.

MRS. LEE: That's terrible. Does this happen very often?

CASHIER: Not at all. In fact, it happens only _____. Unfortunately, this kind of situation _____ the manager's assistance, but he's not here right now.

MRS. LEE: Just when you _____ that something like this won't happen, it does!

CASHIER: I guess I have to figure out your bill by myself. Let's see—the total for your purchases _____ $13.35.

MRS. LEE: Did you _____ my discount coupons?

CASHIER: No, I forgot. Thanks for reminding me.

Collocations

Idioms are expressions made up of words that take on new and different meanings when they are used in combination with one another. Collocations, on the other hand, are simply words that are traditionally used together by native English speakers, so that their combination becomes expected. Unlike idioms, the individual words in collocations retain their own meaning. Collocations can occur in a number of different patterns, including adjective + noun, verb + noun, verb + adverb, noun + verb, and noun + noun.

feel free: go ahead (and do something)

- Please *feel free* to borrow my dictionary any time.

feel funny: feel slightly ill, feel uncomfortable

- I've been *feeling funny* ever since I ate the fish.

- I *feel funny* about turning down that invitation for dinner.

feel like (something): want to have or do something

- I *feel like* eating Indian food tonight.

- I don't *feel like* going to a movie.

get going: move quickly

- We'd better *get going* if we're going to make the next train.

get it: make sense of something

- Suichi just didn't *get it* when Lily told the joke.

out of date: no longer useful or modern

- Your map is so *out of date* that it shows some countries that don't even exist.

out of control: impossible to guide or direct; in a rage

- The car went *out of control* and hit the fence.

- Diego really went *out of control* after he missed the penalty kick.

out of the question: not permitted; not workable

- Taking vacation now is *out of the question* because we have to meet that deadline.

EXERCISES

Fill in the blanks to complete the collocations.

I'll have to get   if I'm going to get to class on time today. Sometimes I just don't feel   going to class at all. But skipping class is out   —I'd get in trouble!

I really like our teacher for the first class. She makes us feil   to contribute in class. I never feel   when I make a mistake there. And she makes the material seem so easy that I almost always get   .

The only thing about her is how she dresses—it's so out   ! I think she gets her clothes from her grandmother!

Review: Lessons 1 to 13

A *Match the idiom in the left column with the definition in the right column. The first one is done for you.*

_d_ 1. for one thing		a. for a reason, deliberately
____ 2. for good		b. temporarily
____ 3. on purpose		c. from the beginning
____ 4. so far		d. for example
____ 5. first-rate		e. punctually
____ 6. right away		f. excellent, superb
____ 7. every other		g. until now
____ 8. for the time being		h. uncomfortable, worried
____ 9. all along		i. very soon, immediately
____ 10. on time		j. modern, current
____ 11. ill at ease		k. alternate
____ 12. up to date		l. permanently, forever

B *In the space provided, mark whether each sentence is true (**T**) or false (**F**).*

1. ____ If you *take your time* getting ready for work in the morning, you do it *in a hurry.*

2. ____ If you have *worn out* your clothes, you would use them to *dress up.*

3. ____ If you have difficulty *getting along with people,* you probably also have trouble *making friends.*

4. ____ If the doctor advises you *to cut down* on work at the office, you should *take some time off.*

5. _____ If you *call it a day,* you are just *waking up* in the morning.

6. _____ If you *get carried away* while *taking a* difficult *hike,* you may *tire out.*

7. _____ If you know some information *by heart,* you still have to *figure it out.*

8. _____ If you *find fault with* a person *over and over again,* that person may choose not *to pay attention to* your criticism.

9. _____ If you *make up your mind* about a problem, you still have to *think* it over.

10. _____ If you *take a trip* to a foreign country, you may want to *brush up on* the language first.

11. _____ If store owners want to *crack down* on shoplifting, they should *spend* more *time* monitoring shoppers.

12. _____ If important decisions always *are up to you,* then you *take turns* making them.

C *Fill in each blank with the appropriate form of the idioms using* **look** *listed below.*

to look at	to look for	to look up
to look out	to look over	to look into

1. Jeff's mother expects him _____ her directly while she is speaking to him.

2. The police detective was very eager _____ the cause of the accident.

3. Harriet went to the library _____ some facts for her research paper.

4. Before the important exam, I _____ my lecture notes for the class.

5. Jason can't seem to locate his car keys. Could you help us _____ them?

6. _____ There's a car coming towards us quickly.

D *Fill in each blank with the appropriate form of the idioms using **take** listed below.*

to take one's time	to take off	to take out
to take part in	to take into account	to take a trip
to take place	to take turns	to take hold of

1. Do you have any idea when the symphony concert is scheduled _____?

2. To drive safely, you should _____ the steering wheel with both hands.

3. You should _____ when you walk on ice. If you hurry, you might fall down.

4. Bill finally _____ the new girl in school. They went to the park together and had a picnic.

5. Many young actors and actresses wanted _____ the theater production of *Hamlet*. Unfortunately, only a few were chosen.

6. Kurt didn't have enough money to pay for dinner because he didn't _____ the cost of the tax and tip.

7. My brother and I _____ doing household chores. One day he washes the dishes, and the next day I do them.

8. Please _____ your shirt and put it in the laundry basket. It's too dirty to wear anymore.

9. This spring the Dobsons are planning _____ to Oregon and Washington state.

E *Fill in each blank with the appropriate form of the idioms using **get** listed below.*

to get in/to get on	to get up	to get to
to get out of/to get off	to get back	to get over
to get along (with)	to get rid of	to get used to

1. I should _____ some of these old papers. If I threw them away, there would be a lot more space in my desk.

2. I didn't like the weather here at first, but after a few months I _____ the rain.

3. Marco got very depressed when his father died. He has just started _____ his sadness.

4. Before we were able _____ the bus to downtown, we had to let the passengers on the bus.

5. Please _____ and _____ the car on the
   driver's side. The door on the passenger side is broken.

6. Felix is such a nice guy that it's easy _____ him.

7. Sarah usually _____ at about six o'clock in the
   morning, _____ work by eight o'clock, and
   _____ home by around six o'clock in the evening.

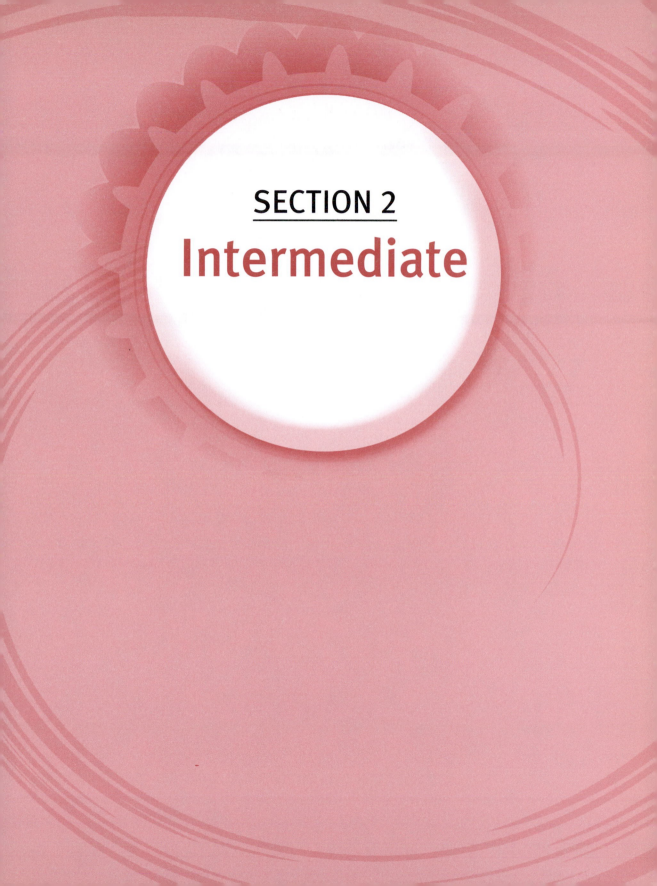

SECTION 2
Intermediate

Lesson 14

to eat in/to eat out: to eat at home/to eat in a restaurant

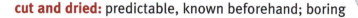

- I feel too tired to go out for dinner. Let's *eat in* again tonight.

- When you *eat out*, what restaurant do you generally go to?

cut and dried: predictable, known beforehand; boring

- The results of the national election were rather *cut and dried*; the Republicans won easily.

- A job on a factory assembly line is certainly *cut and dried*.

to look after: to watch, to supervise, to protect (also: **to take care of, to keep an eye on**)

- Grandma will *look after* the baby while we go to the lecture.

- Who is going to *take care of* your house plants while you are away?

- I'd appreciate it if you'd *keep an eye on* my car while I'm in the store.

to feel like: to have the desire to, to want to consider
This idiom is usually followed by a gerund (the *-ing* form of a verb used as a noun).

- I don't *feel like* studying tonight. Let's go to a basketball game.

- I *feel like* taking a long walk. Would you like to go with me?

once and for all: finally, absolutely

- My daughter told her boyfriend *once and for all* that she wouldn't date him anymore.

- *Once and for all*, John has quit smoking cigarettes.

to hear from: to receive news or information from

To hear from is used for receiving a letter, telephone call, etc., from a person or organization.

- I don't *hear from* my brother very often since he moved to Chicago.

- Have you *heard from* the company about that new job?

to hear of: to know about, to be familiar with; to consider

The second definition is always used in the negative.

- When I asked for directions to Mill Street, the police officer said that she had never *heard of* it.

- I tried to pay Uncle Byron for the movie ticket, but he wouldn't *hear of it.*

to make fun of: to laugh at, to joke about

- They are *making fun* of Carla's new hair style. Don't you think that it's really strange?

- Don't *make fun of* Jose's English. He's doing the best he can.

to come true: to become reality, to prove to be correct

- The weatherman's forecast for today's weather certainly *came true.*

- Everything that the economists predicted about the increased cost of living has *come true.*

as a matter of fact: really, actually (also: **in fact**)

- Hans thinks he knows English well but, *as a matter of fact,* he speaks very poorly.

- I didn't say that. *In fact,* I said quite the opposite.

to have one's way: to arrange matters the way one wants (especially when someone else doesn't want the same way) (also: **to get one's way**)

- My brother always wants to *have his way,* but this time our parents said that we could do what I wanted.

● If Sheila doesn't *get her way*, she becomes very angry.

to look forward to: to expect or anticipate with pleasure
This idiom can be followed by a regular noun or a gerund.

● We're greatly *looking forward* to our vacation in Mexico.

● Meg never *looks forward* to going to work.

EXERCISES

Choose the appropriate idiomatic expression to substitute for the italicized word or words in each sentence below. Idioms from previous lessons are indicated by number.

1. I asked my neighbor *to watch* my dog while I was out of town.
    a. to come to (Lesson 13)
    b. to make fun of
    c. to look after

2. Do you *want to consider* going to a movie tonight?
    a. feel like
    b. stand to reason (Lesson 12)
    c. look forward to

3. I wonder when I'm finally going *to receive news* from Joe.
    a. to hear of
    b. to hear from
    c. to make fun

4. The teacher told her young student, "Please don't cheat *from this time into the future.*"
    a. from now on (Lesson 11)
    b. once and for all
    c. as a matter of fact

5. Aren't you glad that we decided *to eat at a restaurant* tonight? This food is great!

   a. to eat in

   b. to take out (Lesson 3)

   c. to eat out

6. The decision to sell the failing business was rather *predictable.*

   a. come true

   b. in fact

   c. cut and dried

7. Barbara is a nice person, but unfortunately she always has *to arrange matters the way she wants.*

   a. to have her way

   b. to make up her mind (Lesson 5)

   c. to come true

8. Are you *pleasantly anticipating* the end of the school semester?

   a. hearing of

   b. looking forward to

   c. paying attention to (Lesson 8)

9. *Actually,* I really don't want to take a break right now. I'd rather keep working.

   a. Little by little (Lesson 2)

   b. As a matter of fact

   c. For good (Lesson 5)

10. Everything that my parents told me about becoming an adult *proved to be correct.*

    a. came true

    b. to hear of it

    c. in fact

B *Answer these questions orally by making use of the idiomatic expressions studied in this lesson.*

1. What famous American actors and actresses have you *heard of?*
2. If you were a parent, what activity would you *not hear of* your small child doing?
3. When was the last time that you *heard from* an old friend from your childhood?
4. Do you prefer to *eat in* or *eat out?* How often do you eat out?
5. Is there anything that you want to stop doing *once and for all?* What?
6. What event in the near future you *looking forward to?*
7. When might you insist on *having your way* with your friends?
8. How do you feel when other people *make fun of* you?
9. When do you most *feel like* studying—in the morning or in the evening? Why?
10. All people have hopes and desires for the future. What hope or desire do you want most *to come true?*

Lesson 15

inside out: with the inside facing the outside

- Someone should tell that man that his shirt is *inside out*.

- The high winds ruined the umbrella by blowing it *inside out*.

upside down: with the upper side turned toward the lower side

- The accident caused one car to turn *upside down,* its wheels spinning in the air.

- One of the students was only pretending to read her textbook; the teacher could see that the book was actually *upside down*.

to fill in: to write answers in **(S)**; to inform, to tell **(S)**
For the second definition, the idiom can be followed by the preposition *on* and the information that someone is told.

- You should be careful to *fill in* the blanks on the registration form correctly.

- Barry was absent from the meeting, so I'd better *fill* him *in*.

- Has anyone *filled* the boss *in* on the latest public relations disaster?

to fill out: to complete a form **(S)**
This idiom is very similar to the first definition above. *To fill in* refers to completing various parts of a form, while *to fill out* refers to completing a form as one whole item.

- Every prospective employee must *fill out* an application with her name, address, previous jobs, etc.

- The teenager had some trouble *filling* the forms *out* by himself, so his mother helped him.

to take advantage of: to use well, to profit from; to use another person's weaknesses to gain what one wants

- I *took advantage of* my time off from work and went shopping.

- Teddy is such a small, weak child that his friends *take advantage of* him all the time by demanding money and making him do things for them.

no matter: regardless of

This idiom is a shortened form of *it doesn't matter.* It is followed by a question word such as *how, where, when, who,* etc.

- *No matter* how much money he spends on his clothes, he never looks well dressed.

- *No matter* where that escaped prisoner tries to hide, the police will find him.

to take up: to begin to do or study, to undertake **(S)**; to occupy space, time, or energy **(S)**

For the second definition, in instances of time and energy, *take up* is often shortened to *take.*

- I'm going to *take up* sailing. I would have *taken* it *up* when I was younger, but I didn't have the money.

- The piano *takes up* too much space in our living room. However, it would *take* too much time to move it right now; so we'd better wait until later.

to take up with: to consult someone about an important matter **(S)**

The important matter follows the verb *take,* while the person consulted follows *with.*

- Can I *take* the problem *up with* you right now? It's quite urgent.

- I can't help you with this matter. You'll have to *take* it *up with* the manager.

to take after: to resemble a parent or close relative (also: **to look like,** for physical appearance only)

- Which of your parents do you *take after* the most?

- Sam *looks like* his father, but he *takes after* his mother in personality.

in the long run: eventually, after a long period of time
This idiom is similar in meaning to *sooner or later* (Lesson 1).
The difference is that *in the long run* refers to a more extended period of time.

- *In the long run,* the synthetic weave in this carpet will wear better than the woolen one. You won't have to replace it so soon.

- If you work hard at your marriage, you'll find out that, *in the long run,* your spouse can be your best friend in life.

in touch: having contact
This idiom is often followed by *get, be, keep,* or *stay.*

- I haven't been *in touch* with Sabrina since her baby was born. I should get *in touch* with her soon.

- I certainly enjoyed seeing you again after all these years. Let's be sure to keep *in touch.*

out of touch: not having contact; not having knowledge of

- Sonia and I had been *out of touch* for years, but then suddenly she called me the other day.

- Larry has been so busy that he is *out of touch* with world events.

EXERCISES

 Choose the appropriate idiomatic expression to substitute for the italicized word or words in each sentence below. Idioms from previous lessons are indicated by number.

1. It is a fact of life that older children use *the weaknesses of* their younger brothers and sisters.
   a. take up with
   b. out of touch with
   c. take advantage of

2. If you want the water to come out of the bottle, you have to turn it *so the top is where the bottom was with the upper side facing the lower side.*
   a. inside out
   b. in the long run
   c. upside down

3. Jeanne has a determination to do well in every aspect of her work; she never *stops trying* just because the work is difficult.
   a. gives up (Lesson 13)
   b. takes up
   c. takes after

4. *Regardless of* what he says, I don't believe any of the excuses he offers.
   a. As for (Lesson 12)
   b. No matter
   c. As a matter of fact (Lesson 14)

5. Farah just got back from vacation; let's *inform her* on what happened while she was gone.
   a. fill her in
   b. fill her out
   c. think her over (Lesson 4)

6. This assignment is so *boring and predictable* that I'll be finished in a very short time.
   a. out of the question (Lesson 8)
   b. out of touch
   c. cut and dried (Lesson 14)

7. After Misha finished taking art classes, he decided *to begin to study* journalism.
   a. to take up
   b. to take advantage of
   c. to look like

8. Tom and I have been *not having contact* for many years now; I can hardly believe that he just wrote me a letter.

    a. in touch

    b. in the long run

    c. out of touch

9. Whom do you think that Terry *resembles* most—her mother or her father?

    a. look over (Lesson 6)

    b. takes after

    c. fills out

10. The hospital got crowded after a bad case of the flu became widespread in the city.

    a. was carried away (Lesson 11)

    b. took up with

    c. broke out (Lesson 12)

B *Answer these questions orally by making use of the idiomatic expressions studied in this lesson.*

1. Which of your parents do you *take after* in appearance? In personality?
2. What people in your life are you most *in touch* with?
3. Who have you been *out of touch* with for many years?
4. What object *takes up* the most space in your room?
5. What are some good ways that you can *take advantage of* a friend? Some bad ways?
6. What is the difference between *filling* something *in* and *filling* something *out?*
7. When you apply to college or university, what forms do you have to *fill out?*
8. What kind of life do you want for yourself *in the long run?*
9. If a person has serious mental or emotional problems, whom can this person *take* the problems *up with?*
10. For what reasons might someone wear a piece of clothing *inside out?*

Lesson 16

on one's toes: alert, cautious
This idiom is usually used with the verbs *stay* and *keep*.

- It's important for all the players on a soccer team to stay *on their toes*.

- We'd better keep *on our toes* while we're walking along the dark portions of this street.

to watch one's step: to walk or move cautiously, to be careful when walking or moving

- You should *watch your step* when you hike on that trail; it's very steep and dangerous.

- The workers put up a sign that said *"Watch your step!"* to warn people about the hole in the sidewalk.

to watch what one says/does: to speak or behave carefully

- *Watch what you say* about Oliver's weight. He's very sensitive about it.

- If Vasil doesn't *watch what he does*, he's going to get himself into trouble at work.

to see eye to eye: to agree, to concur

- I'm glad that we *see eye to eye* on that matter.

- A husband and wife don't always *see eye to eye* with each other, but a good marriage can survive small disagreements.

to have in mind: to be considering, to be thinking **(S)**

- What style of dress does Lena *have in mind* for her wedding?

- It's up to you what we eat tonight. Do you *have* anything *in mind?*

to keep in mind: to remember, not to forget **(S)** (also: **to bear in mind**)

- Please *keep in mind* that you promised to call Stan around noon.

- I didn't know that Paula doesn't like vegetables. We should *bear* that *in mind* next time we invite her for dinner.

for once: this one time, for only one time

- *For once* I was able to win a game of golf against Steve, who is a much better player than I am.

- Dad, *for once* would you please let me drive the new car?

to go off: to explode; to sound as an alarm; to leave suddenly without explanation

- The accident happened when a box of firecrackers *went off* accidentally.

- For what time did you set the alarm clock *to go off* tomorrow morning?

- Vince *went off* without saying good-bye to anybody; I hope he wasn't angry.

to grow out of: to outgrow, to become too old or too big for; to be a result of

- He still bites his nails now and then, but soon he'll *grow out of* the habit.

- The need for the salary committee *grew out of* worker dissatisfaction with the pay scale.

to make the best of: to do the best that one can in a poor situation

- If we can't find a larger apartment soon, we'll just have to *make the best of* it right here.

- Even though the Martinez family is having financial problems, they *make the best of* everything by enjoying the simple pleasures of life.

to cut off: to shorten by cutting the ends **(S)**; to disconnect or stop suddenly **(S)**

- The rope was two feet longer than we needed, so we *cut off* the extra length.

● My Internet provider *cut off* service today, so I couldn't check my e-mail.

to cut out: to remove by cutting **(S)**; to stop doing something **(S)** (for the second definition, also: **to knock it off**)
For the second definition, the idiom is usually separated by the pronoun *it*.

● The child likes to *cut out* pictures from the newspaper and to paste them in a notebook.

● He kept bothering her, so finally she told him to *cut it out*. However, he wouldn't *knock it off* until her larger brother appeared.

EXERCISES

 Choose the appropriate idiomatic expression to substitute for the italicized word or words in each sentence below. Idioms from previous lessons are indicated by number.

1. My brother and I are having a lot of arguments these days. We can hardly *agree* on anything.

    a. go off

    b. see eye to eye

    c. have in mind

2. My grandmother has to *walk cautiously* when going down stairs.

    a. watch what she says

    b. cut it out

    c. watch her step

3. Will's foot size is now so big that he's already *become too big for* these baseball shoes.

    a. on his toes for

    b. cut off

    c. grown out of

4. *This one time* I'd like to win a million dollars in the state lottery, but I'm sure I won't.

   a. So far (Lesson 4)

   b. For once

   c. All along (Lesson 2)

5. Mira awoke suddenly when her alarm clock *sounded* in the morning.

   a. went on (Lesson 6)

   b. went off

   c. went out (Lesson 8)

6. I can't answer your questions about this problem; go see the supervisor and *consult him about it*.

   a. keep him in mind

   b. take it up with him (Lesson 15)

   c. make the best of him

7. At the end of the break, the teacher had *to suddenly stop* the students' conversations and resume class.

   a. to cut out

   b. to go off

   c. to cut off

8. Even though there are a lot of quiet moments in baseball, the players on the field should always stay *alert*.

   a. in a hurry (Lesson 5)

   b. bearing them in mind

   c. on their toes

9. Sarah's negative attitude about life *is a result of* an unhappy childhood.

   a. makes the best of

   b. grows out of

   c. gets along

10. I don't know what you think, but I *am considering* a pizza party for Billy's birthday.

    a. have in mind

    b. never mind (Lesson 2)

    c. keep in mind

B *Answer these questions orally by making use of the idiomatic expressions studied in this lesson.*

1. Why should you stay *on your toes* while driving a car?

2. In what places or situations must you *watch your step?*

3. Have you ever had to *watch what you said* around someone? Who was the person? What couldn't you say around him/her?

4. What do you do when you don't *see eye to eye* with a friend? Do you usually stay calm or get angry during an argument?

5. What should parents *keep in mind* as they raise their children? Did your parents do this?

6. Is there anything in life that you would like to do just *for once?*

7. At what time in the morning does your alarm clock usually *go off?*

8. Name one or more habits that you had as a child that later you *grew out of.*

9. As a child, did you like to *cut out* pictures from newspapers and magazines? What did you do with them?

10. Why might someone say *"Cut it out!"* to you?

Lesson 17

to blow out: to explode, to go flat (for tires);
to extinguish by blowing **(S)**

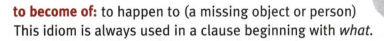

- On our trip to Colorado, one of the car tires *blew out* when it hit a large hole in the road.

- Little Joey wasn't able to *blow* all the candles *out,* so his big sister helped him.

to become of: to happen to (a missing object or person)
This idiom is always used in a clause beginning with *what.*

- What has *become of* my pencil? I had it ten minutes ago, but now I can't find it.

- I wondered what *became of* you. I looked around the shopping center for two hours, but I couldn't find you at all.

to shut up: to close for a period of time **(S)**; to be quiet, to stop talking
The second definition of this idiom is impolite in formal situations.

- During the hurricane, all the store owners *shut* their shops *up.*

- Bob's sister told him to *shut up* and not say anything more about it.

- The student got into big trouble for telling his teacher *to shut up.*

have got: to have, to possess

- Curtis *has got* a bad cold. He's sneezing and coughing a lot.

- How much money *have* you *got* with you right now?

have got to: must (also: **have to**)

- She *has got to* go to Chicago today to sign the contract papers.

- I *have to* be back home by two o'clock or my wife will feel ill at ease.

to keep up with: to maintain the same speed or rate as

- Frieda works so fast that no one in the office can *keep up with* her.

- You'll have to walk more slowly. I can't *keep up with you.*

on the other hand: however, in contrast

- Democracies provide people many freedoms and privileges. *On the other hand,* democracies suffer many serious problems such as crime and unemployment.

- My sister takes after my father in appearance. *On the other hand,* I take after my mother.

to turn down: to reduce in brightness or volume **(S)**; to reject, to refuse **(S)**

- Please *turn down* the radio for me. It's too loud while I'm studying.

- Lola wanted to join the military but the recruiting officer *turned* her application *down* because Lola is hard of hearing in one ear.

fifty-fifty: divided into two equal parts

- Let's go *fifty-fifty* on the cost of a new rug for our apartment.

- The political candidate has a *fifty-fifty* chance of winning the election.

to break in: gradually to prepare something for use that is new and stiff **(S)**; to interrupt (for the second definition, also: **to cut in**); to enter illegally or by force

- It is best to *break* a new car *in* by driving it slowly for the first few hundred miles.

- While Carrie and I were talking, Bill *broke in* to tell me about a telephone call.

- Peter, it's very impolite to *cut in* like that while others are speaking.

- The thief was caught as he tried to *break into* our home.

a lost cause: a hopeless case, a person or situation having no hope of positive change

- It seems that Charles will never listen to our advice. I suppose it's *a lost cause.*

- The police searched for the missing girl for two weeks, but finally gave it up as *a lost cause.*

- People who have committed several crimes and show no sorrow about their actions are generally *lost causes.*

above all: mainly, especially

- *Above all,* don't mention the matter to Gerard; he's the last person we should tell.

- Sheila does well in all her school subjects, but *above all* in mathematics. Her math scores are always over 95 percent.

EXERCISES

 Choose the appropriate idiomatic expression to substitute for the italicized word or words in each sentence below. Idioms from previous lessons are indicated by number.

1. The last racehorse wasn't able *to maintain the same speed as* the other horses in the race.

   a. to keep up with

   b. to cut in

   c. to keep track of (Lesson 11)

2. There's only one piece of pie left. Would you like to share it *in two equal parts?*

   a. above all

   b. fifty-fifty

   c. a lost cause

3. I didn't like that actor's last movie. His new one, *however,* is excellent.

   a. on the other hand

   b. above all

   c. as a matter of fact (Lesson 14)

4. Tell the children *to stop talking* now or they'll get punished.

   a. to blow out

   b. to break in

   c. to shut up

5. What has *happened to* my wallet? I can't find it anywhere.

   a. become of

   b. have to

   c. turned down

6. Jack didn't believe what his parents told him, but all of it has *proved to be correct.*

   a. made a difference (Lesson 3)

   b. a lost cause

   c. come true (Lesson 14)

7. Ted greatly appreciates his wife's concern for him and, *especially,* her love.

   a. above all

   b. on the other hand

   c. at least (Lesson 4)

8. Dr. Hampton *must* leave the office early because he has an urgent appointment at the hospital.

   a. has got

   b. has got to

   c. would rather (Lesson 7)

9. We almost had a serious accident on the highway when the front tire of our car *exploded.*

   a. blew up (Lesson 12)

   b. blew out

   c. tired out (Lesson 2)

10. Joyce never believed that the university would *reject* her application for graduate study.

   a. turn down

   b. break in

   c. throw away (Lesson 8)

B *Answer these questions orally by making use of the idiomatic expressions studied in this lesson.*

1. Have you ever been in a car when a tire *blew out?* What happened?
2. When is it acceptable to tell someone to *shut up?* Not acceptable?
3. Why might a homeowner *shut* his house *up?*
4. How much money *have* you *got* in your wallet or purse right now?
5. What *have* you *got to* do to take care of your health?
6. Have you ever had difficulty *keeping up with* other students in school? Why or why not?
7. For what reasons might a person be *turned down* for a job?
8. Why is it important to *break in* a new vehicle?
9. For what reasons might you think of someone as being *a lost cause?*
10. *Above all,* what is the most important part of your life?

Lesson 18

to do without: survive or exist without something (also: **to go without**)

- With prices so high now, I'll have to *do without* a new suit this year.

- As a traveling salesperson, Monica can't *do without* a car.

- It's a shame that so many poor people in the world have to *go without* basic necessities of life such as nutritious food and suitable shelter.

according to: in the order of; on the authority of

- The students on the football team were ranked *according to* height, from shortest to tallest.

- *According to* my dictionary, you are using that word in your essay incorrectly.

to be bound to: to be certain to, to be sure to
This idiom is used when the occurrence of an event seems inevitable or unavoidable.

- We *are bound to* be late if you don't hurry up.

- With the economy improving now, their business *is bound* to make more money this year.

for sure: without doubt (also: **for certain**)

- In the dark, I couldn't tell *for sure* whether it was Kristina or Dana who drove by.

- I know *for certain* that Gene will move back to Washington next month.

to take for: to perceive or understand as **(S)**
This idiom is usually used when someone is mistakenly perceived. A noun or pronoun must separate the idiom.

- Because of his strong, muscular body, I *took* him *for* a professional athlete. As it turns out, he doesn't play any professional sports.

- What do you *take* me *for*—a fool? I don't believe what you're saying at all.

to try out: to test, to use during a trial period **(S)**; to audition

- I can let you *try* the computer *out* for a few days before you make a decision about buying it.

- Max *tried out* for the role of Hamlet in his school play.

to tear down: to destroy by making flat, to demolish **(S)**

- The construction company had to *tear down* the old hotel in order to build a new office building.

- The owners had to *tear* the house *down* after half of it burned down in a fire.

to tear up: to rip into small pieces **(S)**

- Deirdre *tore up* the letter angrily and threw all the pieces into the trash can.

- He told the lawyer to *tear* the old contract *up* and then to prepare a new one.

to go over: to be appreciated or accepted
This idiom is usually followed by the adverb *well*. (In Lesson 6 this idiom has the meaning *to review,* as in the second sentence of the second example below.)

- The teacher's organized lessons always *go over* well with her students.

- The comedian's jokes weren't *going over* well, and the audience wasn't laughing at all. I think that the comedian should go over his material more carefully before each act.

to run out of: to exhaust the supply of, not to have more of

- We *ran out of* gas right in the middle of the main street in town.

- It's dangerous to *run out of* water if you are in an isolated area.

at heart: basically, fundamentally
This idiom is used to describe the true character of a person.

- Amir sometimes seems quite unfriendly, but *at heart* he's a good person.

- The Fares often don't see eye to eye, but at heart they both love each other very much.

on hand: available, nearby
This idiom is often followed by *in case.*

- I always keep some extra money *on hand* in case I forget to get cash from the bank.

- The concert organizers arranged to have some security guards *on hand* in case there were any problems during the performance.

EXERCISES

 A *Choose the appropriate idiomatic expression to substitute for the italicized word or words in each sentence below. Idioms from previous lessons are indicated by number.*

1. We'll have to use the restrooms on the next floor because the ones on this floor are *not in working condition.*
   a. run out of
   b. torn down
   c. out of order (Lesson 6)

2. Jennifer seems unpleasant at times, but *basically* she's a kind person.
   a. at heart
   b. for sure
   c. according to

3. The salesperson agreed to let me *test* the car for an hour or so to see if I liked it.

   a. try out

   b. tear up

   c. do without

4. Because of his uniform, he was *perceived as* a police officer, but actually he was just a security guard.

   a. taken for

   b. bound to

   c. looked out (Lesson 5)

5. *On the authority of* the courts, essential government workers cannot go on strike or refuse to perform their jobs.

   a. About to (Lesson 8)

   b. According to

   c. As a matter of fact (Lesson 14)

6. Don't you hate to see the city *demolish* those old historic buildings, all in the name of progress?

   a. put out (Lesson 6)

   b. tear down

   c. go without

7. You'd better make sure you have money *available* before you go to the store.

   a. at heart

   b. on the other hand (Lesson 17)

   c. on hand

8. I was *ready to* go to bed when someone knocked on my apartment door.

   a. bound to

   b. about to (Lesson 8)

   c. feel like (Lesson 14)

9. The President's speech *was accepted* so well that all the members of Congress stood up and applauded.

   a. went over

   b. was bound to

   c. found out (Lesson 2)

10. Wes is planning to go with us to Disneyland *without doubt.*

   a. out of the question (Lesson 8)

   b. at last (Lesson 2)

   c. for sure

B *Answer these questions orally by making use of the idiomatic expressions studied in this lesson.*

1. If you lost your job and didn't have much money, what would you have to *do without?*

2. Why are students in some schools placed in classes *according to* ability?

3. If parents want to raise their children well, what are they *bound to* do?

4. If you see a man leaving a house through a window at night, what might you *take him for?*

5. What things would you be sure to *try out* before buying?

6. Why might you feel like *tearing up* a letter or some schoolwork?

7. Have you ever said or done something special that *went over* well? What was it?

8. What should you do if you *run out of* energy while you're studying in the evening?

9. Are you a serious person or a fun-loving person *at heart?*

10. Do you like to keep cash *on hand* for emergencies? How much cash do you keep *on hand?*

Lesson 19

to bite off: to accept as a responsibility or task
This idiom is often used when one accepts more responsibility than one can handle alone. It is usually used in the form *to bite off more than one can chew.*

- When I accepted the position of chairman, I didn't realize how much I was *biting off.*

- When Tran registered for 18 units in his last semester at college, he *bit off more than he could chew.*

to tell apart: to distinguish between
(also: **to tell from**) **(S)**

- The two brothers look so much alike that few people can *tell* them *apart.*

- Most new cars are very similar in appearance. It's almost impossible to *tell* one *from* another.

all in all: considering everything

- There were a few problems, but *all in all* it was a well-organized seminar.

- Leo got a low grade in one subject, but *all in all* he's a good student.

to pass out: to distribute (also: **to hand out**) **(S)**; to lose consciousness
The verbal idiom *to hand out* can be made into the noun **handout** to refer to items that are distributed.

- Please help me *pass out* these test papers. It would take an hour to *hand* them *out* by myself.

- Alright, students, here are the class *handouts* for this week.

- The weather was so hot in the soccer stadium that some of the fans in the stands *passed out.*

to go around: to be sufficient or adequate for everyone present; to circulate, to move from place to place

- We thought that we had bought enough food and drink for the party, but actually there wasn't enough to *go around*.

- There's a bad strain of influenza *going around* right now. Have you gotten your flu shots yet?

- Gabriel has been *going around* telling people that he was accepted to Harvard University. Do you believe him?

to be in the/one's way: to block or obstruct; not to be helpful, to cause inconvenience (for both, also: **to get in the/one's way**)

- Jocelyn couldn't drive through the busy intersection because a big truck *was in the way*.

- Our small child tried to help us paint the house, but actually he just *got in our way*.

to put on: to gain (pounds or weight) **(S)**; to present, to perform **(S)**

- Bob has *put on* a lot of weight recently. He must have *put* at least fifteen pounds *on*.

- The Youth Actor's Guild *put on* a wonderful version of "Romeo and Juliet" at the Globe Theater.

to put up: to construct, to erect **(S)**; to lift, to raise upwards **(S)**

- The construction company is tearing down that old office building in order to *put up* a new one.

- The store owner *put up* a sign listing the store's hours.

to put up with: to tolerate, to accept unwillingly

- The employee was fired because his boss could not *put up with* his mistakes any longer.

- While I'm studying, I can't *put up with* any noise or other distractions.

in vain: useless, without the desired result

- All the doctors' efforts to save the injured woman were *in vain*. She died three hours after being admitted to the hospital.

- We tried *in vain* to reach you last night. Is your phone out of order?

day in and day out: continuously, constantly (also: **day after day**; for longer periods of time, **year in and year out** and **year after year**)

- During the month of April, it rained *day in and day out*.

- *Day after day* I waited for a letter from him, but one never came.

- *Year in and year out*, the weather in San Diego is the best in the nation.

to catch up: to work with the purpose of fulfilling a requirement or being equal to others
The idiom is often followed by the preposition *with* and a noun phrase. It is similar in meaning to *to keep up with* from Lesson 17.

- The student was absent from class so long that it took her a long time *to catch up*.

- If you are not equal to others, first you have *to catch up with* them before you can *keep up with* them.

EXERCISES

A *Choose the appropriate idiomatic expression to substitute for the italicized word or words in each sentence below. Idioms from previous lessons are indicated by number.*

1. News *circulated* the office that the company president was being forced to resign.

   a. went over (Lesson 18)

   b. went around

   c. went on (Lesson 6)

2. I'm sorry that I have to *interrupt* while you're talking, but there's an important phone call for you, Mr. Mason.

   a. break in (Lesson 17)

   b. be in the way

   c. put up with

3. Several students had not been able to keep up with the rest of the class, so they had a lot of difficulty *working to be equal to* the others.

   a. putting on

   b. catching up

   c. putting up

4. Marsha's efforts to open the door were *useless;* it was tightly shut.

   a. all in all

   b. in vain

   c. no matter (Lesson 15)

5. Jens didn't know anything about carpentry, so he only *caused inconvenience* when he tried to help Tom build a storage room.

   a. put up

   b. passed out

   c. got in the way

6. Get in touch with me when you *return* from your trip, okay?

   a. get back (Lesson 5)

   b. go around

   c. tell from

7. *Considering everything,* I'm lucky to have a steady job, even if it isn't very exciting.

   a. All in all

   b. At all (Lesson 4)

   c. Day in and day out

8. The Lawsons couldn't *tolerate* the noise of the busy highway next to their house any longer, so they decided to move.

    a. put up

    b. put up with

    c. put out (Lesson 6)

9. Are there enough snacks *to be sufficient for everyone,* or should we drive down to the store for more?

    a. to pass out

    b. to go around

    c. bite off

10. The magician *performed* an amazing act for the audience of young people.

    a. bit off

    b. called for (Lesson 13)

    c. put on

B *Answer these questions orally by making use of the idiomatic expressions studied in this lesson.*

1. Have you ever *bitten off more than you could chew?* Explain the situation.
2. In what part of the world is it difficult to *tell* night and day *apart?*
3. Have you ever *passed out* or seen someone *pass out?* What happened?
4. What do people in an audience have to do if there are not enough seats to *go around?*
5. What should you tell someone who is *in your way* while you're working?
6. How could someone *put on* a lot of weight in a short time?
7. In class, when would you *put up* your hand? Is this easy or difficult for you to do? Why?
8. What are some of the things in life that you have trouble *putting up with?*
9. How would you feel if you had to stay at home *day in and day out* taking care of the housework and, perhaps, children? Would you feel satisfied or would you feel unhappy? Explain your reasons.
10. Have you ever found yourself *catching up* with others? What was the situation?

Lesson 20

to hold still: not to move **(S)**

- Please *hold still* while I adjust your tie.

- If you don't *hold* that camera *still,* you'll get a blurred picture.

to break the news: to deliver new, usually upsetting, information

- I hated to *break the news* to Adam that he was fired from his job.

- This morning, the radio station *broke the news* that the president had died.

to be the matter: to be unsatisfactory, to be improper, to be wrong
In a question, this idiom is used with *what* or *something.* In an answer, *something* or *nothing* is usually used.

- A: What *is the matter,* Corrine? You look very upset.

- B: Yes, something *is the matter.* I've lost my purse!

- A: *Is something the matter,* Chet? You don't look well.

- B: No, nothing *is the matter.* I'm just a little under the weather.

to bring up: to rear, to raise from childhood **(S)**; to mention, to raise an issue, to introduce a topic **(S)**

- Parents should *bring up* their children to be responsible members of society.

- Jung wanted to *bring* the scheduling problem *up* at the club meeting, but finally she decided against doing so.

- One of the students *brought up* an interesting point related to the subject in our textbook.

to get lost: to become lost; to go away in order not to bother
The second definition provides a very informal, even rude, meaning that should be used only with close friends. It is usually used in a joking manner.

- While driving in Boston, we *got lost* and drove many miles in the wrong direction.

- Todd kept bothering me while I was studying, so I told him to *get lost*.

to hold up: to delay, to make late **(S)**; to remain high in quality; to rob

- A big accident *held up* traffic on the highway for several hours.

- Deidre is amazed at how well her car has *held up* over the years.

- A robber *held up* the local bank yesterday.

to run away: to leave without permission, to escape

- The young couple *ran away* and got married because their parents wouldn't permit it.

- That cat *runs away* from anyone who tries to come near!

to rule out: to refuse to consider, to eliminate **(S)**

- Heather *ruled out* applying to college in Texas because she would rather go to school in Canada.

- I'd like to watch a good movie on TV tonight, but a ton of homework *rules* that *out*.

by far: by a great margin, clearly

- Jacquie is *by far* the most intelligent student in our class.

- This is *by far* the hottest, most humid summer we've had in years.

to see off: to say good-bye upon departure by train, airplane, bus, etc.
(also: **to send off**) **(S)**
A noun or pronoun must divide the idiom.

- We are going to the airport to *see* Peter *off* on his trip to Europe.

- When I left for Cincinnati on a business trip, no one came to the train station to *send* me *off*.

to see out: to accompany a person out of a house, building, etc. **(S)**
A noun or pronoun must again divide the idiom.

- The Johnsons were certain to *see* their guests *out* as each one left the party.

- Would you please *see* me *out* to the car? It's very dark outside.

no wonder: it's no surprise that, not surprisingly
This idiom derives from reducing *it is no wonder that . . .*

- *No wonder* the portable heater doesn't work. It's not plugged into the electrical outlet!

- Jacques has been out of town for several weeks. *No wonder* we haven't seen him recently.

EXERCISES

A *Choose the appropriate idiomatic expression to substitute for the italicized word or words in each sentence below. Idioms from previous lessons are indicated by number.*

1. This new microwave isn't *remaining high in quality* as well as the microwave that I had for over ten years.
   a. holding still
   b. bringing up
   c. holding up

2. When Tim's roommate asked to borrow Tim's car for the whole weekend, Tim responded jokingly by saying, *"Go away!"*

    a. Get lost

    b. Rule out

    c. Never mind (Lesson 2)

3. The Simpson children were *raised* on a farm, so they have an appreciation of nature that most children don't have.

    a. put up (Lesson 19)

    b. brought up

    c. held up

4. Would you like Alex *to accompany you outside* to your car?

    a. to see you off

    b. to see you out

    c. to see you about (Lesson 10)

5. This is the best meal I've ever had in this restaurant *by a great margin.*

    a. by far

    b. little by little (Lesson 2)

    c. by myself (Lesson 3)

6. The police *eliminated* the celebrity as a suspect in the murder case when they learned that he was out of town at the time of the crime.

    a. brought up

    b. ruled out

    c. saw out

7. *It's no surprise that* the soup is cold. No one turned on the stove!

    a. No matter (Lesson 15)

    b. Nothing is the matter

    c. No wonder

8. I'm sorry I'm late. I was *delayed* by heavy traffic.

    a. taken hold of (Lesson 11)

    b. held up

    c. held still

9. The new flight attendant hesitated *to raise* the issue of overtime pay with the union representative.

    a. to bring up

    b. to be the matter of

    c. to be in charge of (Lesson 9)

10. *Occasionally* Mary enjoys driving up to the mountains and camping by herself.

    a. Over and over again (Lesson 8)

    b. Every now and then (Lesson 10)

    c. Once in a blue moon (Lesson 13)

B *Answer these questions orally by making use of the idiomatic expressions studied in this lesson.*

1. Give an example of when you would have to *hold still*.
2. Has anyone ever *broken the news* of something sad to you? How did you respond?
3. Where were you brought up? Did your parents *bring* you *up* well?
4. Are there any topics that you would never *bring up* with your parents? Can you mention any of them?
5. Have you ever *gotten* seriously *lost?* What happened?
6. Could you ever tell someone to *get lost?* Why or why not?
7. Which countries manufacture products that generally *hold up* well?
8. What kind of job would you definitely *rule out* for yourself? Why?
9. When was the last time that someone *saw* you *off?*
10. Why would you offer to *see* someone *out* of your house or apartment?

Lesson 21

to go up: to increase; to be constructed, to be erected
The second definition is the same as the one for *to put up* in Lesson 19, except that *to go up* is not used with a noun object.

- Economists are predicting that consumer prices *are going up*.

- A new office *is going up* in the downtown area. A major construction company is *putting it up*.

to go up to: to approach (also: **to come up to, to walk up to, to run up to, to drive up to,** etc.)
The related forms have the same meaning, but the type of movement is different.

- After the lecture, several people in the audience *went up to* the speaker to congratulate her.

- The little girl *came up to* me and talked to me as if she had known me for years.

- Bill's friend didn't want to admit that they had gotten lost, but finally he agreed to *drive up to* a gas station and inquire about the correct route.

to hand in: to submit or deliver something that is due **(S)**

- Every student has to *hand in* an original composition each week of the semester.

- All the salespeople *hand* their weekly reports *in* on Friday.

in case: in order to be prepared if (something happens)
When the idiom occurs at the end of the sentence (as in the second example), then the meaning is *in order to be prepared if something happens*. The "something" might be an accident, a delay, etc.

- You'd better close the windows *in case* it rains.

- We should be sure to leave for the airport early, just *in case*.

to take apart: to disassemble, to separate the parts of something **(S)**
A noun or pronoun usually divides this idiom.

- It is much easier to *take* a watch *apart* than it is to assemble it.

- The engine had a serious problem, so the mechanic had to *take* it *apart* completely in order to fix it.

to put together: to assemble **(S)**
A noun or pronoun usually divides this idiom. The preposition *back* is used when something has been broken or disassembled and then is being reassembled, as in the second example.

- Todd followed the directions on the box but he couldn't manage to *put* the bicycle *together* properly.

- After the teenager took the broken video game apart and fixed it, he was unable to *put* it *back together* again.

to be better off: to be in a more favorable condition or situation
The opposite of this idiom is **to be worse off**.

- Jim would *be better off* staying at home because of his cold.

- You'd *be* much *better off* working in an office than in a factory.

- The economies of some nations *are worse off* than they were several decades ago.

to be well-off: to have enough money to enjoy a comfortable life, to be rich
(also: **to be well-to-do**)

- They live in the best section of town in a large home; they *are* very *well-off*.

- By the time I reach the age of fifty-five, I hope to *be well-to-do* and to travel frequently.

to take by surprise: to surprise, to amaze, to astonish **(S)**
A noun or pronoun usually divides this idiom.

- The offer of a high-paying position with another company *took* me *by surprise*.

- The president's announcement that the university was in financial trouble didn't *take* anyone *by surprise*.

to stress out: to worry, be anxious, or feel stress; to cause to worry, be anxious, or feel stress **(S)**

- Samantha is *stressing out* because her son is sick. Once his health improves, she'll feel much better too.

- Lance doesn't like to go over his finances because money matters *stress* him *out*.

to name after: to give the same name as another **(S)**

- Helen's parents *named* Helen *after* her grandmother.

- My grandson is *named after* Calvin Coolidge, the 30th President of the United States.

to hold on: to grasp tightly or firmly; to wait, to be patient (also: **to hang on**)
The second definition is often used when someone is talking on the telephone.

- The little girl *held on* to her mother's hand and refused to let go as they walked through the large crowd of people.

- (on the telephone) Could you please *hold on* a moment while I get a pencil and paper?

- *Hang on,* Miranda, I'm not ready to go yet.

EXERCISES

A *Choose the appropriate idiomatic expression to substitute for the italicized word or words in each sentence below. Idioms from previous lessons are indicated by number.*

1. In some countries, *being rich* means just having a home for your family.
   a. being worse off
   b. being well-off
   c. being up to (Lesson 11)

2. Jake was *astonished* when he learned that he had been accepted to Yale University.
   a. taken by surprise
   b. taken apart
   c. better off

3. We'd better take umbrellas with us *to be prepared if* it rains.
   a. on the other hand (Lesson 17)
   b. in case
   c. in time to (Lesson 7)

4. Surono wasn't able *to submit* his assignment to the teacher because he had forgotten to do it.
   a. to put together
   b. to pass out (Lesson 19)
   c. to hand in

5. Suki is afraid to fly, so airplane trips really *cause her to worry*.
   a. take her apart
   b. take her by surprise
   c. stress her out

6. Dr. Madison has *assembled* an excellent team of administrators and instructors for the staff of the new community college.

    a. put together

    b. taken apart

    c. gone up

7. Timmy, I asked you *to be patient* a moment while I finish getting dressed.

    a. to take hold of (Lesson 11)

    b. to hold on

    c. to stress out

8. I can't believe how prices are increasing more and more every year.

    a. going up to

    b. going up

    c. going off (Lesson 16)

9. Richard went to the library to locate information on the Civil War.

    a. to look up (Lesson 4)

    b. to look out (Lesson 5)

    c. to look after (Lesson 14)

10. When most men get lost, they are uncomfortable *approaching* other people to ask for directions.

    a. going up

    b. stressing out

    c. going up to

B *Answer these questions orally by making use of the idiomatic expressions studied in this lesson.*

1. Is the cost of living *going up* in your country? What factors can cause prices to go up?

2. Have you ever *gone up to* a famous person and asked for an autograph? (An *autograph* is the signature of a famous person.)

3. Do you always *hand in* assignments in class on time, or are you sometimes late? Do you ever forget to *hand* them *in?*

4. Do you keep any supplies on hand *in case* of an emergency? For which types of emergencies are you prepared?

5. As a child, did you enjoy *taking* things *apart?* What kinds of things did you *take apart?*

6. After you took them apart, did you always *put* them *together* again? Were you always successful?

7. Are you *better off* now than you were five years ago? How?

8. Do you consider yourself *well-off?* If not, do you expect to be *well-off* in the future? How do you expect to accomplish it?

9. Do you enjoy being *taken by surprise* or do surprises make you uncomfortable?

10. Are you *named after* somebody? Who?

Lesson 22

to stop by: to visit or stop somewhere briefly (also: **to drop by**, **to drop in on**)
To drop by and *to drop in on* are used for visits that are unplanned or unexpected.

- Let's *stop by* the supermarket and pick up a few grocery items.

- Since we're in the neighborhood, let's *drop by* Jiro's house. Do you think he'd mind if we *dropped in on* him?

to drop (someone) a line: to write a note to someone **(S)**

- As soon as I get to Florida, I'll *drop* you *a line* and tell you about my new job.

- If you have time, *drop* me *a line* now and then while you're traveling.

to give (someone) a call: to telephone **(S)**
(also: **to call**)

- I'll *give* Hakim *a call* tomorrow to invite him to the party.

- *Call me* tomorrow, Jane. We'll arrange a time to have lunch together.

to come across: to meet or find unexpectedly
(also: **to run across**); to be perceived or judged as
(also: **to come off**)

- While Cheryl was cleaning the attic, she *came across* some very old coins. It took her by surprise to *run across* something like that.

- Jeff's boss *comes across* as a tough, unpleasant person, but actually Jeff says that he is a good employer.

- Some people *come off* quite differently than they really are.

to cross one's mind: to come to one's thoughts unexpectedly or briefly, to occur to one

- It didn't *cross my mind* to invite Rachelle to the party until it had already started.

- The thought of visiting Spain *crossed my mind*, but I went to Turkey instead.

to stand for: to represent, to signify; to tolerate
The second definition is usually used in a negative sense.
The meaning is the same as *to put up with* in Lesson 19.

- On the American flag, each star *stands for* one of the fifty states, and each stripe stands for one of the original thirteen colonies of the 1800s.

- The citizens wouldn't *stand for* the increase in crime in their city, so they hired more police officers and built another jail.

to stand a chance: to have the possibility of accomplishing something
This idiom is often used with an adjective such as *good* or *excellent*. It also occurs in the negative, sometimes with the adjective *much*.

- The New York baseball team *stands a good chance* of winning the World Series this year.

- Because John doesn't have any previous work experience, he doesn't *stand a chance* of getting that job.

- The woman injured in the serious train accident doesn't *stand much chance* of surviving.

to look on: to watch as a spectator, to observe

- Hundreds of people were *looking on* as the police and firefighters rescued the passengers in the wrecked train.

- I stayed with my son at his first soccer practice and *looked on* as the coach worked with the boys.

EXERCISES

A *Choose the appropriate idiomatic expression to substitute for the italicized word or words in each sentence below. Idioms from previous lessons are indicated by number.*

1. In computer code, a binary number such as 10010001 *represents* a letter, number, or other character on a computer keyboard.
   a. stands for
   b. looks on
   c. figures out (Lesson 7)

2. As John fell asleep, it *occurred to him* that he hadn't fed his cat.
   a. made an impression on him (Lesson 10)
   b. gave him a call
   c. crossed his mind

3. I haven't heard from Ally lately; maybe I should *telephone* her tonight.
   a. look up to her
   b. give her a call
   c. keep her in mind (Lesson 16)

4. Rhonda has *to briefly visit* the pharmacy in order to get her medication.
   a. to stop by
   b. to pull off
   c. to come across

5. Did Frida *write you* after she returned to Germany?
   a. look down on you
   b. drop you a line
   c. look up to you

to look up to: to admire, to respect greatly

- Children will most certainly *look up to* their parents if the children are brought up well.

- Everyone *looks up to* the director of our department because he is a kind and generous person.

to look down on: to feel superior to, to think of someone as less important

- People who are in positions of power should be careful not to *look down on* those who work for them.

- Why does Alma *look down on* Mario just because his family is so poor?

to take off: to leave the ground (for airplanes); to leave, often in a hurry
The noun form **takeoff** derives from this idiom.

- The plane *took off* over an hour late. The passengers had to buckle their seatbelts during takeoff.

- Do you have *to take off* already? You just arrived an hour ago!

to pull off: to succeed in doing something difficult **(S)**; to exit to the side of a road (also: **to pull over**)

- The group of investors *pulled off* a big deal by buying half the stock in that company. I wonder how they *pulled* it *off* before the company could prevent it.

- The motorist *pulled off* the road when the police officer turned on the red lights and the siren.

- If you get a flat tire while driving, you should *pull over* right away.

6. How can you *tolerate* such a mess in your son's bedroom? You should make him wash all those dirty clothes and clean up his room!

   a. put away (Lesson 4)

   b. look down on

   c. stand for

7. The crowd of political supporters was *anxious* on the night of the election.

   a. taken off

   b. stressed out (Lesson 21)

   c. looked on

8. While Jerry was walking down the sidewalk, he *unexpectedly found* a twenty-dollar bill lying by the side of the road.

   a. came across

   b. came to (Lesson 13)

   c. took off

9. Leah managed *to succeed in winning* an important victory in a statewide track and field competition this year, even though no one expected her to do so.

   a. to come off

   b. to pull off

   c. to take off

10. However, I'm afraid that Leah doesn't *have the possibility* of winning a medal in the Olympic Games next year.

    a. stand a chance

    b. stand for

    c. stand to reason (Lesson 12)

B *Answer these questions orally by making use of the idiomatic expressions studied in this lesson.*

1. If you had to buy a birthday card, what kind of store would you *stop by?*

2. Are you always certain to *drop* your friends *a line* when you travel? Why or why not?

3. What would you do if you *came across* a bag containing a large amount of money?

4. When giving a talk or lecture to an audience, how would a speaker want to *come across?*

5. What do the initials U.S.A. *stand for?* Are there initials that *stand for* your country? What are they?

6. What kind of person *stands a chance* of becoming a country's leader? (consider a president, king, dictator, etc.)

7. Do you prefer to be involved in playing a sport or just *looking on?* Why?

8. Whom do you *look up to* most in life? Why?

9. What kind of a person would you *look down on?* Should you avoid feeling this way, or is it sometimes all right?

10. When might you want to, or have to, *take off* from a party early? Have you ever done this?

Lesson 23

to make do: to manage, to cope
This idiom is used when a person must accept a substitute that is not the most suitable.

- Pearl doesn't have a clean shirt so she has to *make do* with the one she wore yesterday.

- During difficult economic times, many people have to *make do* with less.

to give birth to: to bear a human being or animal

- Jane's mother has just *given birth to* twin girls.

- The zoo's Siberian tiger just *gave birth to* a baby cub.

close call: a situation involving a narrow escape from danger (also: **close shave**)

- We had a *close call* when a small fire in our kitchen almost spread to the rest of the house.

- Bob, that car nearly hit us! What a *close shave!*

to get on one's nerves: to annoy or disturb (also: **to bug**)

- Laura loves to talk to anyone. Sometimes her chatter really *gets on my nerves*.

- Jack asked his neighbor to turn down the stereo because it was *bugging* him and he couldn't concentrate.

to put down: to suppress, to quell **(S)**; to criticize unfairly **(S)**

- The police arrived just in time to *put down* the disturbance before it got very serious.

- Fred tries his best at playing tennis. You shouldn't *put* him *down* like that.

to go for: to be sold at a certain price; to seek or strive for; to agree with or to consider
The third definition is similar to *to feel like* (Lesson 14).

- This dress probably *goes for* about $50, don't you think?

- Peter was *going for* first place in the swim meet, but he wasn't able to do better than third place.

- You can ask Ava to give you the money, but I doubt that she'll *go for* it.

to be into: to have as an interest, such as a sport or hobby (also: **to get into**) **(S)**

- What sports *are* you *into?* I don't have any time to get into sports.

to stay up: to remain awake, not to go to bed

- I want to *stay up* tonight and watch a late movie on TV.

- He *stays up* every night until after one o'clock, preparing his homework.

to stay in: to remain at home, not to go out
An idiom with the opposite meaning is **to stay out**.

- On a rainy day, I like to *stay in* and read.

- Young people are able to *stay out* late at night and get very little sleep.

to take over: to assume control or responsibility for **(S)**; to do or perform again **(S)**
The meaning of the second definition is almost the same as *do over* in Lesson 11. Also for the second definition, a noun or pronoun must divide the idiom.

- That large investment company specializes in *taking over* smaller businesses that are in financial trouble.

- Most students didn't do well on the important test, so the instructor let them *take* it *over.*

- Little Mikey didn't have much chance to hit the baseball during practice, so the coach let him *take* his turn *over.*

to show up: to appear, to arrive; to be found or located (also for the second definition: **to turn up**)

- It really gets on my nerves that Ursula *shows up* late for every meeting.

- Willie hopes that the watch he lost last Sunday *shows up* soon.

- We've looked everywhere for that book, but it hasn't *turned up* yet.

to clean out: to empty, to tidy by removing **(S)**; to steal, to rob **(S)**; to buy or purchase all of something **(S)**

- It's time to *clean out* your closet so that you'll have more storage space.

- A burglar entered my apartment while I was gone and *cleaned* me *out*. He took over $200 in cash and jewelry.

- Thousands of shoppers *cleaned out* the store that was selling all its products at very reduced prices.

EXERCISES

A *Choose the appropriate idiomatic expression to substitute for the italicized word or words in each sentence below. Idioms from previous lessons are indicated by number.*

1. The instructor allowed the student *to do* the class *again* because he had received a bad grade the first time.
   a. to do without (Lesson 18)
   b. to make do
   c. to take over

2. Last night my husband and I *remained awake* until after midnight waiting for our daughter to return from a date.
   a. stayed in
   b. stayed up
   c. showed up

3. David doesn't *have a possibility* of winning enough money in Las Vegas to buy a new car. He's just wasting his money by gambling.

   a. have a close call

   b. stand a chance (Lesson 22)

   c. be better off (Lesson 21)

4. We should get our refrigerator repaired soon. The rattling noise really *disturbs me.*

   a. turns me up

   b. puts me down

   c. gets on my nerves

5. Mr. Fulsom was late leaving his office because a last-minute telephone call *delayed him.*

   a. took him over

   b. held him up (Lesson 20)

   c. went in for him

6. Thousands of customers cleaned out the department store because everything *was being sold for* a very cheap price.

   a. was going for

   b. was into

   c. was coming to (Lesson 13)

7. The other students in Judy's class *criticize her unfairly* because she enjoys doing homework and helping the teacher.

   a. put her down

   b. get on her nerves

   c. take her apart (Lesson 21)

8. Are there enough sandwiches *to be sufficient for everyone,* or should I go to the kitchen to make more?

    a. to get into

    b. to make do

    c. to go around (Lesson 19)

9. When Ralph *arrives,* we'll discuss the matter of the missing funds.

    a. cleans out

    b. shows up

    c. stays in

10. I can't believe what a *narrow escape* it was when the car went off the road and passed within a few feet of us.

    a. lost cause (Lesson 17)

    b. first-rate (Lesson 10)

    c. close call

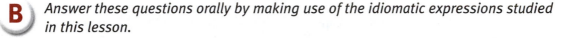

B *Answer these questions orally by making use of the idiomatic expressions studied in this lesson.*

1. If your car was broken but you still needed to get to work, how would you *make do?*

2. Describe a *close call* that you, or someone you know, has had.

3. When might babies or small children *get on your nerves?*

4. What sports or hobbies *are* you *into?*

5. How late do you usually *stay up?*

6. Why might you decide to *stay in* instead of going out?

7. For what reasons might large businesses *take over* smaller businesses?

8. Why would someone have to *take* a class *over?* Has this ever happened to you?

9. In the United States, when should you generally *show up* for a business meeting? When should you *show up* for a casual party?

10. What would be a good reason for *cleaning out* a garage?

Lesson 24

to knock out: to make unconscious **(S)**
The noun form **knockout** derives from this idiom.

- The prizefighter *knocked out* his opponent with one punch in the first five seconds of the first round.

- It was the fastest *knockout* in boxing history.

to knock oneself out: to work very hard (sometimes too hard) to do something
A reflexive pronoun must divide the idiom.

- She really *knocked herself out* trying to pass that difficult class.

- Don't *knock* yourself *out* during practice. Save your strength for the competition later.

to carry out: to accomplish, to execute **(S)** (also: **to go through with**)

- It's easy to make a plan for losing weight, but it's always much harder to *carry* it *out*.

- Charles promised to *go through with* his plan to enroll in graduate school and get an advanced degree.

to run into: to meet someone unexpectedly; to crash or collide into
(also: **to bump into**)

- It was a shock to *run into* an old friend from high school when I was on vacation last month.

- The drunk driver was slightly injured when he *ran into* a telephone pole.

to set out: to start traveling toward a place (also: **to set off, to head out**); to arrange or display neatly (also: **to lay out**) **(S)**

- We *set out* for the top of the mountain at dawn.

- Unfortunately, as we *set off,* it started to snow heavily, so we decided to head out again later.

- The children tried to *set out* the dishes on the table, but their dad had to help to *lay them out* properly.

to set out to: to intend to, to act purposefully to

- We *set out to* paint the house in one day, but quickly realized that it would be impossible to do so.

- Janet *set out* to compete for the large scholarship grant by writing a good essay.

to draw up: to prepare documents or legal papers **(S)**

- Our lawyer agreed to draw up the contract next month. We had hoped he would *draw it up* sooner than that.

give and take: compromise, cooperation between people

- *Give and take* is an important element of a successful marriage.

- Most business negotiations involve *give and take* between the parties involved.

to drop out of: to stop attending; to withdraw from
This idiom can be made into the noun form **dropout.**

- Some students *drop out of* secondary school early in order to get jobs. However, such dropouts often regret their decision later in life.

- Two more baseball teams have *dropped out of* the youth league due to a lack of players.

to believe in: to accept as true, have faith in

- Some people *believe in* being honest in all human affairs, while others accept the need to lie in order to get one's way.

- Throughout the history of man, some cultures have *believed in* one god while others have believed in the existence of many gods.

to cheer up: to make happier, to feel less sad **(S)**

- We all tried to *cheer up* the little boy when he started to cry.

- After the death of Deanne's husband, it was difficult to *cheer* her *up* at all.

to make sense: to be sensible or reasonable

- It *makes sense* to wait until a sunny day to visit the park together.

- That Jimmy ran away from home suddenly doesn't *make sense* to any of us.

EXERCISES

 A *Choose the appropriate idiomatic expression to substitute for the italicized word or words in each sentence below. Idioms from previous lessons are indicated by number.*

1. Alberto *has faith in* his own ability to succeed in his new business enterprise.
   a. is in charge of (Lesson 9)
   b. carries out
   c. believes in

2. *Cooperation* is important in all relationships between people, especially those who must live and work together closely.
   a. Making sense
   b. Seeing eye to eye (Lesson 16)
   c. Give and take

3. Cynthia *intended to* finish her term paper in one day, but actually it took her three days.

    a. went through with

    b. set out to

    c. knocked herself out to

4. The bicyclist *collided with* a wall and was scraped up badly.

    a. ran into

    b. run out of (Lesson 18)

    c. put up with (Lesson 19)

5. The student apologized to his teacher for *submitting* the essay late.

    a. handing in (Lesson 21)

    b. dropping out of

    c. carrying out

6. In order to avoid the early morning rush hour traffic, we *started traveling* before down.

    a. laid out

    b. set out

    c. went out (Lesson 8)

7. My friends tried *to make me feel happier* when I learned that I couldn't graduate because I had to take one class over.

    a. to make me sense

    b. to cheer me up

    c. to change my mind (Lesson 5)

8. It *isn't reasonable* to ruin one's health by drinking alcohol and smoking cigarettes.

    a. doesn't make a difference (Lesson 3)

    b. doesn't make up your mind (Lesson 5)

    c. doesn't make sense

9. Peter *raised* an important issue regarding the next soccer tournament at the club meeting.

    a. put up (Lesson 19)

    b. brought up (Lesson 20)

    c. drew up

10. Stacy *worked very hard* to prepare a nice meal for her family at their reunion.

    a. set out

    b. carried out

    c. knocked herself out

B *Answer these questions orally by making use of the idiomatic expressions studied in this lesson.*

1. Have you ever been *knocked out?* What happened?
2. Have you ever *knocked yourself out* to accomplish something? What was it?
3. When you set goals for yourself, do you usually *carry* them *out?*
4. When was the last time that you *ran into* someone from your past?
5. Why should a store be careful in how it *sets out* its product displays?
6. Have you *drawn up* a will? Why is it important to do so?
7. Why might an athlete *drop out of* a sporting event? Has this ever happened to you?
8. Do you *believe in* capitalism as an economic system? Why or why not?
9. If someone has just lost a job, what could you do or say to *cheer* him or her *up?*
10. For some people, it *makes sense* to spend most of the extra income they make. Would this be true for you? Why or why not?

Lesson 25

to burst out: to depart quickly (also: **to storm out**); to act suddenly
For the second definition, this idiom is usually followed by a gerund form such as *laughing, crying, singing,* etc.

- Faye and Debbie were so angry at each other that one of them *burst out* the front door of the house and the other *stormed out* the back door.

- It was so funny to see a little baby in the audience *burst out* crying when the choir group *burst out* singing at the start of the recital.

to get away: to get free, to escape

- We always try to *get away* from the noise and heat of the city for a month or two each summer.

- No one knows how the suspected criminal *got away* from the police.

to get away with: to avoid punishment for

- Jonathan tries to *get away with* coming late to work almost every day; someday he'll suffer the consequences.

- Terence can't continue to put his friends down like that and expect to *get away with* it forever.

to serve (someone) right: to receive one's just punishment **(S)**
This idiom is usually used at the beginning of a sentence after the subject *it*. Compare the following examples with those in the previous idiom above.

- It *serves* Jonathan *right* to be fired from his job.

- It *serves* Terence *right* that none of his friends are willing to hang out with him anymore.

to keep up: to prevent from sleeping **(S)**; to continue maintaining (speed, level of work, condition, etc.) **(S)**

- Could you please turn down the TV volume? You're *keeping up* the children.

- If we can *keep up* this speed, we should arrive there in about two hours.

- James is so proud of his daughter for getting mostly A's in school. He's certain that she can *keep up* the good work.

- The Federal Reserve Bank hopes to *keep* the value of the dollar *up* at least through the rest of the year.

to keep up with: to have current knowledge of; to understand as an explanation
This idiom should be compared to the meaning of *to keep up with* in Lesson 17.

- Evan *keeps up with* world affairs by reading a news magazine each week.

- I understand a lot of the Spanish language, but I can't *keep up with* the fast conversation in this Mexican film.

to stand out: to be easily visible or noticeable (also: **to stick out**)
This idiom is used for someone or something that is different from all others.

- Her bright red hair makes her *stand out* from others in the group.

- Brandon Styles is a tall, distinguished gentleman who *sticks out* in any crowd.

to let on: to reveal or tell what you know, to hint

- We are going to the movies tonight and we don't want Doris to go. If you see her, make sure not to *let on*.

- They asked me not *to let on* to Ted that we're planning the birthday party; it's supposed to be a big surprise.

to go wrong: to fail, to result badly

- Something *went wrong* with the engine, so we had to have the car towed to a garage.

- Shawn should have been here over an hour ago; I'm certain that something *went wrong*.

to meet (someone) halfway: to compromise with someone

- Steve wanted $4,500 for his car, and Gwen offered $4,000. They *met* each other *halfway* and agreed on $4,250.

- After a long process of give and take, the owners of the company agreed to *meet* the workers *halfway* by providing some additional health benefits but no wage increase.

to check up on: to examine with the purpose of determining condition
(also: **to check on**)
The noun form **checkup** derives from this idiom.

- The government always *checks up on* the background of employees who are hired for sensitive military projects.

- The doctor wants me to have a thorough medical *checkup* as part of a preventive medicine program.

to stick up: to point or place upwards **(S)**; to rob **(S)**
The second definition of this idiom has the same meaning as the third definition of *to hold up* (Lesson 20).

- You should put some water on your hair. It's *sticking up* in the back.

- A masked thief *stuck up* a grocery store in the neighborhood last night.

EXERCISES

A

Choose the appropriate idiomatic expression to substitute for the italicized word or words in each sentence below. Idioms from previous lessons are indicated by number.

1. That professor lectures so quickly that I have trouble *understanding his explanations.*
   a. keeping him up
   b. checking up on him
   c. keeping up with him

2. We hope *to escape* this weekend for some camping in the mountains.
   a. to get away with
   b. to break out (Lesson 12)
   c. to get away

3. That man's purple pants and pink shirt really *are noticeable* from a long distance.
   a. stand out
   b. keep up
   c. stop by (Lesson 22)

4. The government was forced *to assume control of* a failing financial institution.
   a. to take over (Lesson 23)
   b. to burst out
   c. to go wrong

5. You should really *compromise with Sally* and agree to share the cost of the car repairs.
   a. serve Sally right
   b. meet Sally halfway
   c. check on Sally

6. How do you manage *to have current knowledge of* political affairs when you're so busy working?

   a. to let on

   b. to keep up with

   c. to be in charge of (Lesson 9)

7. *Considering everything,* we did a very good job of building that storage room by ourselves.

   a. All along (Lesson 2)

   b. Letting on

   c. All in all (Lesson 19).

8. The heat and humidity *prevented me from sleeping* late into the night.

   a. kept me up

   b. stuck me up

   c. cut me off (Lesson 16)

9. No one in the audience reacted to the comedian's first joke except Tamara, who *acted suddenly by* laughing.

   a. got away with

   b. cut down on (Lesson 9)

   c. burst out

10. Please be sure not *to reveal* that we already know about Hal's upcoming retirement. He hasn't officially announced it yet.

    a. to let on

    b. to stick out

    c. to storm out

B *Answer these questions orally by making use of the idiomatic expressions studied in this lesson.*

1. Why might you *burst out* of a place such as a room, office, apartment, house, etc?

2. What do you like to do when you *get away* for a while?

3. As a child, what did you try to *get away with?* Did you usually succeed, or did your parents usually catch you?

4. Some people think that it *serves someone right* to receive the death penalty for the crime of murder. Do you agree or disagree?

5. What might *keep* you *up* at night? Do you usually go to sleep easily or with difficulty?

6. Do you try to *keep up with* world events? What is your preferred source of information?

7. In the room that you are in right now, what *stands out the* most?

8. What could *go wrong* during a travel tour of a foreign country?

9. Are you ever willing to *meet* someone *halfway* even after you have made up your mind about something? Why or why not?

10. Why is it important for a doctor to *check up on* your health? Do you go to the doctor regularly for a checkup?

Lesson 26

to come about: to happen

- I didn't find any explanation in the newspaper about how the political coup *came about*.

- The flood *came about* as a result of the heavy winter rains.

to bring about: to cause to happen
This idiom is used to indicate *who* or *what* caused something to come about.

- John *brought about* the accident because of his carelessness.

- The heavy rains we have each spring *bring about* serious flooding.

to build up: to increase slowly, to make stronger gradually **(S)**

- They *built up* their savings account so that they could buy a new house.

- The professional athlete exercises regularly to *build* her strength *up*.

to die down: to decrease, to lessen in strength or intensity

- The hurricane became a less serious tropical storm when its winds *died down*.

- We let the fire in the fireplace *die down* and enjoyed watching the embers as they glowed in the dark.

to fade away: to diminish gradually in time or distance

- The memory of that unpleasant experience has slowly *faded away*.

- The music of the band gradually *faded away* as the parade passed down the street.

to die out: not to exist anymore; to be in the process of disappearing

- Scientists still are not sure exactly why the dinosaurs *died out*.

- That strange, new style of dancing is slowly *dying out*.

to make out: to read or see clearly **(S)**; to prepare a legal document, such as a will, a check, etc. **(S)**

- The letter was so poorly handwritten that I couldn't *make out* many of the words.

- Harold, please *make* the check *out* to Acme Piano Company.

to live up to: to fulfill (a standard or promise)

- It was clear that the lazy student would never *live up to* his family's expectations.

- It surprised us that the car salesperson *lived up to* all the promises he made.

to stick to: to adhere to (a promise), to follow or obey (a set of rules, procedures, etc.)

- He made a promise to his wife to quit smoking and drinking, and so far he has *stuck to* it.

- All organizations expect their employees to *stick to* established work rules and procedures.

- If you try hard to *stick to* your principles, then you'll be able to live up to them.

to rip off: to cheat, to take unfair advantage of
The noun form *ripoff* derives this idiom.

- The car dealership certainly *ripped me off* when I bought this car. It has caused me trouble constantly.

- You paid over $400 for that jacket? What *a ripoff!*

to stand up for: to insist on, to demand; to defend, to support

- If you don't *stand up for* your rights in court, the lawyers will try to stick it to you.

- Frank *stood up for* his friend, who was being put down by other teenagers.

to cut corners: to economize, to save money

- Most students live on limited budgets and have to *cut corners* whenever possible.

- The Livingstons have nine children, so it is essential that they *cut corners* at all times.

EXERCISES

 Choose the appropriate idiomatic expression to substitute for the italicized word or words in each sentence below. Idioms from previous lessons are indicated by number.

1. The other workers *defended* their co-worker who was accused of stealing from the factory warehouse.
   a. stuck to
   b. stood up for
   c. built up

2. It *is sensible* to check at several dealerships for the best price for a new car model.
   a. makes it clear (Lesson 13)
   b. makes out
   c. makes sense (Lesson 24)

3. The army *fulfilled* the commanders' expectations by defeating the enemy.
   a. lived up to
   b. ripped off
   c. counted on (Lesson 6)

4. Memories of my youth gradually *diminish* as I grow older.

    a. fade away

    b. build up

    c. come about

5. Some species of animals will *not exist anymore* unless human beings act to save them.

    a. die down

    b. die out

    c. tire out (Lesson 2)

6. After a long illness, Mr. Felson needed time *to slowly increase* his strength again.

    a. to get better (Lesson 7)

    b. to bring about

    c. to build up

7. You can *profit from* the knowledge of an experienced teacher like Tony in improving your own skills.

    a. take advantage of (Lesson 15)

    b. make out

    c. look into (Lesson 11)

8. When Mrs. Tieg lost her job, the Tieg family had *to economize* in order to survive financially.

    a. to rip off

    b. to cut corners

    c. to tear up (Lesson 18)

9. How did your marketing trip to Asia *result?*

    a. come about

    b. turn out (Lesson 13)

    c. bring about

10. The elderly woman couldn't renew her driver's license because she couldn't *read clearly* the letters on the sign during the vision test.

    a. come about

    b. look after (Lesson 14)

    c. make out

B *Answer these questions orally by making use of the idiomatic expressions studied in this lesson.*

1. How did it *come about* that you are using this book to study idioms?
2. How could someone *bring about* a serious car accident? Has this ever happened to you?
3. Why is it important to *build up* your knowledge of idiomatic expressions?
4. What could cause your love for someone to *die down?*
5. What is an interesting memory of your childhood that has not *faded away?*
6. Should people be concerned about animal and plant species that are *dying out?* Why or why not?
7. How can people correct their vision if they have trouble *making out* things at a far distance?
8. What is the difference between *sticking to* a promise and *living up to* it?
9. How do citizens *stand up for* their country?
10. How might you *cut corners* if you had to do so?

Lesson 27

to take on: to employ, to hire **(S)**; to accept responsibility for, to undertake

- That factory is *taking* a lot of new employees *on* for its new production line.

- Would you be willing to *take on* the task of organizing the next company picnic?

to take down: to remove from an elevated place **(S)**; to write what is said, to note
The first definition of this idiom has the opposite meaning of the second definition *to put up* (Lesson 19).

- We should *take* the pictures *down* from the wall and clean off the dust.

- The secretary *took down* everything that was said at the meeting.

to fall through: to fail to materialize, not to succeed
This idiom is usually used with the noun *plan* or *plans* as the subject.

- Our plan to travel to Europe last summer *fell through* when we were unable to save up enough money.

- Felix made plans to have a party for everyone in his office, but they *fell through* at the last moment.

to fall behind: to lag, to fail to keep up (also: **to get behind**)
This idiom has the opposite meaning of the second definition of *to keep up* (Lesson 25).

- Eve *fell behind* in her studies and finally had to drop out of school.

- If you *get behind* in your car payments, the finance company may repossess it from you.

to give in: to surrender, to stop resisting

- Completely surrounded by our soldiers, the enemy finally gave in.

- Management *gave in* to the strikers' demands and agreed to a shortened work week.

to give off: to release, to produce, to release

- When water boils, it *gives off* steam.

- The flowers in this garden *give off* a lovely scent.

to give out: to distribute; to become exhausted or depleted (also: **to run out**)
The first definition has the same meaning as the first definition of *to pass out* (Lesson 19).

- An usher stood at the door of the theater *giving out* programs.

- I couldn't finish the ten-mile race because my energy *gave out*.

- Jeff plans to travel through South America until his money *runs out*.

to have it in for: to want revenge on, to feel hostile towards (also: **to hold a grudge against**)

- Martina expects to lose her job because her boss has *had it in for* her for a long time.

- The teacher has *held a grudge against* Al ever since the time that he insulted her in front of the class.

to have it out with: to quarrel with, to confront

- I am going to *have it out with* Jack about all the times that he has told us lies.

- Ben *had it out with* his roommate about coming back home so late and making a lot of noise.

to hold off: to delay, or to be delayed, in occurring **(S)**
This idiom has the same meaning as *to put off* (Lesson 5) when a noun or pronoun is used as an object, as in the second example.

- If the rain *holds off* for a few more days, they can finish planting the rest of the crop.

- The judge agreed to *hold off* his decision until new evidence could be introduced into court.

to hold out: to endure, to be sufficient; to survive by resisting; to persist in one's efforts

The first definition for *to hold out* has the opposite meaning of the second definition for *to give out* (seventh idiom, this lesson).

- If our supply of food and water *holds out*, we plan to camp here for another week. However, whenever it *gives out*, we'll have to leave.

- That nation's troops cannot *hold out* much longer against the superior forces of the enemy.

- The valuable football player *held out* for more money before signing a new contract with his team.

to hold over: to extend, to keep for a longer time **(S)**

- They are going to *hold over* that movie for another week because so many people are coming to see it.

- Let's *hold* discussion of this problem *over* until our next meeting.

EXERCISES

A

Choose the appropriate idiomatic expression to substitute for the italicized word or words in each sentence below. Idioms from previous lessons are indicated by number.

1. The traveling circus was so popular in our city that it was *kept for a longer time*.
   a. held out
   b. held off
   c. held over

2. Please put the trash outside; it's *producing* a terrible smell in here.
   a. giving off
   b. giving out
   c. giving in

3. I'm really sorry that your plans to travel to New Zealand *failed to materialize.*

   a. fell behind

   b. fell through

   c. did without (Lesson 18)

4. Would Mary be willing *to undertake* a new project even though she's overloaded with work?

   a. to take down

   b. to take on

   c. to take up with (Lesson 15)

5. Please don't *reveal* that you have knowledge of that secret contractual agreement.

   a. take down

   b. give in

   c. let on (Lesson 25)

6. The campers lost on the high mountain were able *to survive* against the cold weather by building a fire and keeping together.

   a. to hold still (Lesson 20)

   b. to hold out

   c. to put out (Lesson 6)

7. I can't attend class tonight, so would you mind *writing notes on* what the instructor says?

   a. running out

   b. taking down

   c. pointing out (Lesson 7)

8. The committee *delayed* deciding when to have the next board election.

   a. held off

   b. fell behind

   c. called off (Lesson 5)

9. My boss hasn't spoken to me in a week. I wonder if he *feels hostile toward* me because of our disagreement about the labor negotiations.

    a. has it in for

    b. has it out with

    c. holds out

10. The rescue team reached the miners trapped deep in the earth before their small supply of air *became exhausted.*

    a. fell behind

    b. burned out (Lesson 12)

    c. gave out

B *Answer these questions orally by making use of the idiomatic expressions studied in this lesson.*

1. What responsibilities do parents *take on* when they decide to have children?

2. Why is it advisable to *take down* what is said during important discussions or talks?

3. When was the last time that an event or plan *fell through* for you?

4. Do you usually *fall behind* in your work, or do you usually keep up with it? Why?

5. When you *have it out with* a friend, do you usually stick to your opinion or do you often *give in?* Why?

6. What are the possible dangers of the pollution that factories *give off?*

7. When you exercise heavily, does your energy quickly *give out?* Why or why not?

8. Have you ever *had it in for* someone? How did you feel, or what did you do?

9. When you *have it out with* someone, do you usually show your emotions clearly, or do you stay calm and control them?

10. How long can a human being *hold out* without food? Without water?

Collocations

Idioms are expressions made up of words that take on new and different meanings when they are used in combination with one another. Collocations, on the other hand, are simply words that are traditionally used together by native English speakers, so that their combination becomes expected. Unlike idioms, the individual words in collocations retain their own meaning. Collocations can occur in a number of different patterns, including adjective + noun, verb + noun, verb + adverb, noun + verb, and noun + noun.

take care: pay close attention to make sure something bad, like an accident, doesn't happen

- The roads are really icy, so *take care* driving.

take a look: read or consider something quickly, especially in order to decide what to do

- Can you *take a look* at this proposal so we can discuss it in the meeting?

take place: occur

- The meeting *took place* in New York City.

take sides: choose to support a particular opinion or person

- I don't want to *take sides* when you two argue—I think you're both right!

take your pick: select one of two or more things offered

- There's vanilla, chocolate, and strawberry—*take your pick*.

break a habit: stop doing something that you have done regularly for a long time, often something harmful

- It took a long time for João to *break the habit* of staying up until two in the morning—he'd been doing it since he was in his teens!

break the law: disobey a law

- When Dana crossed the street against the red light, she actually *broke the law.*

break a story: be the first to write or distribute a piece of news

- *Nightly News* was the first program to *break the story* about the company's financial problems.

EXERCISES

Fill in the blanks to complete the collocations.

I wasn't sure where the meeting would take , but I knew that it would be the next morning. We were going to talk about the problems the company was having. I wasn't sure whether I should take in the dispute between the president and the financial manager—all I knew was that it looked like somebody had broken , and I didn't want to be a part of it. Frankly, I thought either one of them could have done it— take .

Before the meeting, I wanted to take at the files so I would be familiar with them. What I saw really troubled me. I know it's hard to break when you've been doing it for a long time, but someone should have made these managers stop a long time ago. It was only a matter of time before some news reporter would break . I decided I would go to the meeting, but I would really take not to say anything to cause trouble.

Review: Lessons 14 to 27

A *Match the idiom in the left column with the definition in the right column.*

_____ 1. once and for all   a. in order to be prepared if

_____ 2. lost cause   b. especially, mainly

_____ 3. all in all   c. hopeless situation

_____ 4. by far   d. eventually

_____ 5. give and take   e. clearly, by a great margin

_____ 6. in touch   f. for only one time

_____ 7. above all   g. compromise, cooperation

_____ 8. in the long run   h. basically, fundamentally

_____ 9. close call   i. finally, absolutely

_____ 10. in case   j. narrow escape from danger

_____ 11. for once   k. considering everything

_____ 12. at heart   l. having contact

B *In the space provided, mark whether each sentence is true (T) or false (F).*

1. _____ If a friend doesn't want you *to make fun of* him, the friend might tell you to *shut up*.

2. _____ If you *run into* someone at the store, you are *sticking to* an appointment.

3. _____ If you agree to meet someone *fifty-fifty*, it becomes a matter of *give and take*.

4. _____ If you want to keep *in touch* with someone, you might decide *to stop by* their place for a while.

5. ____ If someone *cuts corners* to save money, she probably *does without* things she would like to have.

6. ____ If you *fall behind* in your studies because you don't try to *keep up with* the other students, *it serves you right*.

7. ____ If something *is going wrong* with your car, then it is *holding up* well.

8. ____ If someone is *very well-off*, the person probably has to *cut corners*.

9. ____ If you haven't *heard from someone* in a long time, you might *drop* the person a *line*.

10. ____ If you are really *into* a certain sport, you might *set out* to be the best you can at it.

11. ____ If you don't want to *make do* without something during an emergency, you should keep it *on hand*.

12. ____ If a repairman were trying to fix a complicated watch, he would *hold still* while *taking* it *apart*.

C Fill in each blank with the appropriate form of the idioms using **call** listed below. Some expressions come from Lessons 1 to 13.

to call	to call for	close call
to call it a day	to call off	

1. It was a _____ when the tire blew out on the busy highway.

2. We _____ early because we had been working since six o'clock in the morning.

3. This recipe _____ cream, but there isn't any in the refrigerator. I'll have to stop by the store and pick up some.

4. Soo _____ her boyfriend in Korea almost every day. The phone bill is her biggest expense.

D *Fill in each blank with the appropriate form of the idioms using **make** listed below. Some expressions come from Lessons 1 to 14.*

to make the best of	to make fun of	to make do
to make sense	to make out	to make good time
to make a difference	to make sure	to make clear

1. It doesn't _____ to me where we eat out tonight. It's your decision.

2. Children love _____ each other by joking and teasing.

3. It took the Petersons only two hours to go from downtown Los Angeles to San Diego by car. They really _____ on that trip.

4. Could you help me understand this lesson? It doesn't _____ to me.

5. The recipe calls for butter, but I don't have any. I'll just have _____ with margarine.

6. When you leave the house, _____ to look the front door.

7. Cheryl couldn't _____ the letters on the sign in the distance because it was getting too dark.

8. Did you _____ it _____ to Deborah that she's not welcome at the dinner party? She'd better not show up.

9. There's nothing we can do at this point to change the unfortunate situation. We'll just have _____ it and go on from here.

E *Fill in each blank with the appropriate form of the idioms using **put** listed below. Some expressions come from Lessons 1 to 14.*

to put on	to put away	to put off
to put out	to put down	to put up with
to put together		

1. Johnny, before you can go outside to play, you have _____ all the toys and clothes on the floor of your room.

2. There's too much noise in here for me to study. I can't _____ it any longer.

3. It's quite cold tonight. I think we should _____ some warmer clothing before we go outside.

4. Please _____ your cigarette in the ashtray immediately. No smoking is allowed in here.

5. I can't _____ doing that important assignment any longer. It's due in just three days.

6. The military troops used force _____ the mass demonstration against the corrupt government.

7. Shari's father helped _____ her new bicycle, which came in pieces in a box.

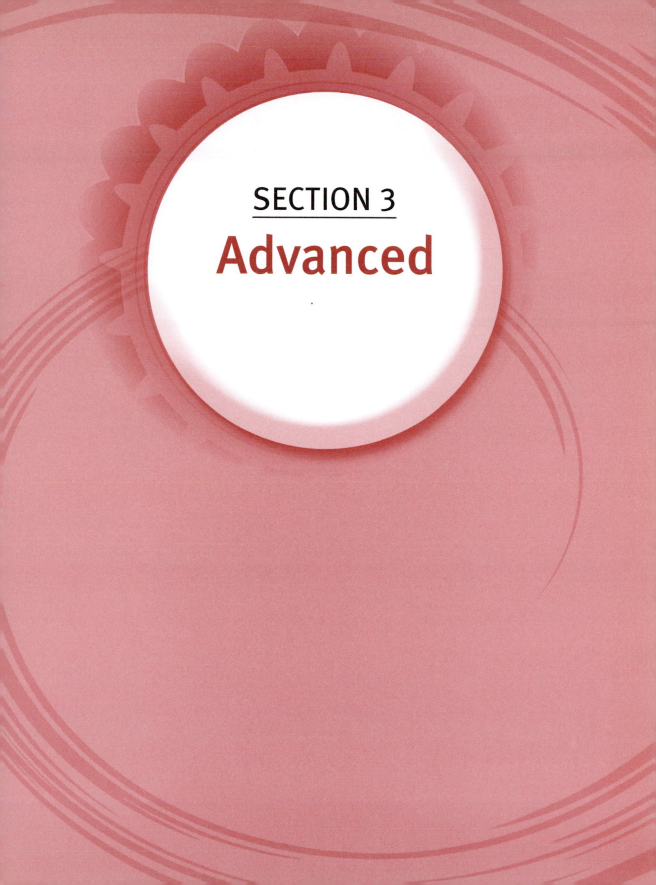

SECTION 3

Advanced

Lesson 28

to let up: to slacken, to lessen in intensity; to relax or ease one's effort (also: related idiom: **to take it easy**)

- If the rain doesn't *let up* soon, we won't be able to have our picnic.

- When Jane is working, she never *lets up* for a moment.

- Jane should *take it easy* or she'll get exhausted.

to lay off: to abstain from or reduce the amount of; to release or discharge from a job (also: related idiom: **to let go**) **(S)**

- If you're trying to lose weight, you should *lay off* sweet things.

- If business continues to be slow, we will have to *lay off* some workers.

- It will be necessary to *let* the newest employees *go* first.

to bring out: to show or introduce (to the public) **(S)**; to make available **(S)**

- Most automobile companies *bring out* new models each year.

- My mother *brought* some snacks *out* for my friends and me to have.

to bring back: to return a bought or borrowed item (also: **to take back**) **(S)**
To bring back is used when you are speaking at the place that an item is bought or borrowed; *to take back* is used when speaking at another place.

- Our store policy is that you can *bring back* the dress as long as you have your sales receipt.

- You can borrow my car if you promise to *bring* it *back* by six o'clock.

- I have to *take* this book *back* to the library today.

to wait up for: to wait until late at night without going to bed

- Don't *wait up for* me. I may be back after midnight.

- We *waited up for* our son until 11:45 P.M. before we called the police.

to leave (someone or something) alone: not to disturb, to stay away from **(S)**
(also: **to let alone**)

- *Leave* the baby *alone* for a while and she may go to sleep.

- After the cat had scratched Peter twice, he *let* it *alone*.

let alone: and certainly not (also: **much less, not to mention**)
Let alone is used after negative forms. The example that follows *let alone* is much less possible than the example that precedes *let alone*.

- I'm too sick today to walk home, *let alone* to go to the zoo with you.

- He doesn't even speak his own language well, *much less* French.

to break off: to terminate, to discontinue **(S)**

- After war began, the two countries *broke off* diplomatic relations.

- Elsa and Bob were once engaged, but they have *broken* it *off*.

to wear off: to disappear gradually

- My headache isn't serious. It will *wear off* after an hour or so.

- The effect of the painkilling drug didn't *wear off* for several hours.

to wear down: to become worn gradually through use (also: **to wear away,**
to wear through) **(S)**
Compare with **to wear out** (to become useless from wear) in Lesson 8.

- If you drag your feet while you walk, you'll *wear down* your shoes quickly.

- The pounding of ocean waves against the coast gradually *wears* it *away*.

- Johnny has *worn through* the seat of his pants.

on the whole: in general, in most ways (also: **for the most part**)

- He is, *on the whole,* a good student.

- *For the most part,* I agree with your suggestions.

touch and go: risky, uncertain until the end

- The complicated medical operation was *touch and go* for several hours.

- The outcome of the soccer final was *touch and go* for the entire match.

EXERCISES

 A Substitute an idiomatic expression for the word or words in italics, making any necessary grammatical changes as well. Then complete each sentence appropriately with your own idea. Also try to use idioms from previous lessons.

1. Mary *discontinued* her relationship with Paul because she couldn't . . .

   Mary broke off her relationship with Paul because she couldn't put up with him anymore.

2. The effect of the medicine *disappeared gradually* after I . . .

3. I think that we should *wait without going to bed* for our daughter until she . . .

4. *In general,* it is best for a student learning English to . . .

5. The company was forced *to release* hundreds of workers because business . . .

6. Sir, you can *return* your jacket to the store if you . . .

7. The outcome of the 100-meter race was *uncertain* because the four runners . . .

8. I have no time to visit the park, *and certainly not* the . . .

9. If the snowstorm doesn't *slacken,* we won't be able to . . .

10. I want you *not to disturb me* so that I . . .

B *Answer these questions orally by making use of the idiomatic expressions studied in this lesson.*

1. If you want to keep a favorite pair of shoes, what can you do when the sole (bottom) of the shoes *wears down?*

2. Have you ever been worried and had to *wait up for* someone? Why was the person late?

3. Why do automobile companies *bring out* new car models each year?

4. In your country, is it possible *to take back* an item to a store after you have bought it?

5. Why is it important *to let up* if you have been working for several hours without a break?

6. Give an example of when you should *leave* a child *alone.*

7. Why should smokers *lay off* smoking cigarettes?

8. How long does it take for the effects of a drug such as alcohol *to wear off?*

9. For what reasons would one country *break off* relations with another country?

10. *On the whole,* what is your favorite music?

Lesson 29

to work out: to exercise; to develop, to devise (a plan); to proceed or end successfully **(S)**
The noun form **workout** derives from the first definition of this idiom.

- Jane *works out* at the fitness center every other morning before going to school. She gets a good *workout* there.

- The advertising department *worked out* a plan to increase company sales.

- We couldn't come up with a good plan for solving the problem, but we agreed to *work* it *out* at a later date.

- Blake's sketches for his engineering project look incorrect. I doubt it will *work out*.

to back up: to drive or go backwards **(S)**; to defend, to support **(S)**; to return to a previous thought

- I couldn't *back* my car *up* because there was a bicycle in the driveway behind me.

- Kyoko asked her friends to *back* her *up* when she went court to fight her speeding ticket.

- Wait a minute. Could you *back up* and say that again?

to back out: to drive a vehicle out of a parking space **(S)**; to withdraw support, to fail to fulfill a promise or obligation

- The parking lot attendant had to *back* another car *out* before he could get to mine.

- We were all ready to sign the contracts when one of the parties to the agreement *backed out*.

to have one's heart set on: to desire greatly, to be determined to

- She *has her heart set on* taking a trip abroad. She's been thinking about it for months.

Todd *has his heart set on* going to medical school and becoming a doctor.

to buy up: to buy the complete stock of **(S)**

Before the hurricane struck, residents *bought up* all the food and water in local stores.

The government plans to *buy up* all surplus grain in order to stabilize the price.

to buy out: to purchase a business or company **(S)**; to purchase all of a person's shares or stock **(S)**
This idiom is similar in meaning to *to take over* in Lesson 23.

Larger companies often *buy out* smaller companies that are having financial difficulties.

Mr. Lee has been trying for some time to *buy* his partner *out* so that he can control the company by himself.

to sell out: to sell all items **(S)**; to arrange for the sale of a company or business **(S)**; to abandon one's beliefs or principles for money or success

That store is closing its doors for good and is *selling out* everything this weekend.

If my new business enterprise is successful, I'll *sell* it *out* for a few million dollars.

The politician *sold out* when he changed political parties to win the election.

to catch on: to become popular or widespread; to understand, to appreciate a joke
This idiom is often used with the preposition *to* for the second definition.

Fashions of the past often *catch on* again among young people.

When the teacher speaks quickly like that, can you *catch on* easily?

His joke was very funny at the time, but when I told it to others later, nobody seemed to *catch on*. I had to tell the joke again before anyone could *catch on to* it.

to be cut out for: to have the necessary skills or talent for
This idiom is most often used in the negative or in questions.

- John *is* certainly not *cut out for* the work of a trial lawyer.

- Are you certain that you *are cut out for* that kind of job?

to throw out: to discard **(S)**; to remove by force **(S)**; to refuse to consider, to reject **(S)**

- Instead of *throwing out* our paper waste in the office, we should recycle it.

- When a fight broke out between two people on the dance floor, the management *threw* them *out*.

- The judge *threw* the case *out* because there was not enough evidence against the defendant.

to throw up: to erect or construct quickly **(S)**; to vomit **(S)**

- The Red Cross *threw up* temporary shelters for the homeless victims of the earthquake.

- The ill patient is unable to digest her food properly, so she is *throwing* all of it *up*.

to clear up: to make understandable (also: **to straighten out**) **(S)**; to become sunny

- The teacher tried *to clear up* our confusion about the meaning of the difficult paragraph in the reading.

- It's rather cloudy this morning. Do you think that it will *clear up* later?

EXERCISES

A *Substitute an idiomatic expression for the word or words in italics, making any necessary grammatical changes as well. Then complete each sentence appropriately with your own idea. Also try to use idioms from previous lessons.*

1. After Jane *exercised* for an hour at the gym, she . . .

2. Larry *defended* his friend who was accused of . . .

3. The company *withdrew support for* the joint venture when . . .

4. This weekend I really *am determined to* . . .

5. That company will have to *sell all its items* if . . .

6. When a new product *becomes popular,* stores should . . .

7. I don't think that Felix *has the necessary talent for* parenthood because he . . .

8. Instead of *discarding* newspapers and plastics, people should . . .

9. The teacher tried to *make understandable* the problem in class, but the students . . .

10. If the weather *becomes sunny* this afternoon, we'll . . .

B *Answer these questions orally by making use of the idiomatic expressions studied in this lesson.*

1. Do you enjoy *working out?* If so, where do you do it? What are some important reasons for *working out?*
2. When you are telling a complicated story to someone, when might you have to *back up?*
3. When you *back out* of a driveway, what do you have to be careful of?
4. Is there anything at the moment that you *have your heart set on?* What is it?
5. If you can't *catch on to* a joke, but everyone else does, what do you do?
6. Do you think that you would be *cut out for* the job of politician? Why or why not?
7. Do you *throw out* items of clothing when they are worn out, or do you find ways to reuse them? Give examples of how some items might be reused.
8. For what reason might a person be *thrown out* of a party?
9. What are some possible causes of a person having to *throw up?*
10. Suppose that you have a serious misunderstanding with a friend. When would you want to *clear up* the misunderstanding right away, and when would you let some time pass by before *straightening* it *out?*

Lesson 30

to slow down: to go, or cause to go, more slowly **(S)**
This idiom can be used both with and without an object.

- The car was going so fast that the driver couldn't *slow* it *down* enough to make the sharp curve.

- You're eating too fast to digest your food well. *Slow down!*

to dry up: to lose, or cause to lose, all moisture **(S)**; to be depleted

- Every summer the extreme heat in this valley *dries* the stream *up*.

- All funds for the project *dried up* when the local government faced a budget crisis.

to dry out: to lose, or cause to lose, moisture gradually **(S)**; to stop drinking alcohol in excess (also: **to sober up**)

- Martha hung the towel outside on the clothesline in order to *dry it out*.

- Some people go to alcohol recovery centers in order to *dry out*.

to be up to (something): to be doing something; to be planning or plotting something, scheming
The first definition usually takes the form of a question.

- Hi, Jake. I haven't seen you in a long time. What have you *been up to?*

- Those boys hiding behind the building must *be up to* something bad.

to beat around the bush: to avoid discussing directly, to evade the issue

- Our boss *beats around the bush* so much that no one in the office knows exactly what he wants us to do.

- Instead of *beating around the bush,* Melinda explained her objection in very clear terms.

to come to an end: to end, to stop
This idiom is used with *finally* and *never* when some activity lasts too long.

- The meeting finally *came to an end* at ten o'clock in the evening.

- Even though my friend seemed to enjoy the movie, I thought that it would never *come to an end.*

to put an end to: to cause to end, to terminate in a definite manner
(also: **to do away with**)

- The dictatorial government *put an end to* organized opposition in the country by making it illegal to form a political party.

- It may never be possible to *do away with* all forms of prejudice and discrimination in the world.

to get even with: to seek revenge, to retaliate
This idiom is similar in meaning to *to have it in for* (Lesson 27).

- Bill has had it in for his boss for a long time. He told me he's planning to *get even with* his boss by giving some company secrets to a competitor.

- I want to *get even with* Steve for beating me so badly in tennis last time. The scores were 6–1 and 6–2.

to fool around: to waste time (also: **to screw around; to goof off, to goof around**); joke, not to be serious

- The teacher got angry because her students were *fooling around* and couldn't finish their class work. She told them that they'd have to stay after school if they continued to *goof off.*

- Sometimes I wish that Pat would stop *fooling around* so much and talk about something more interesting to others.

to look out on: to face, to overlook
The noun form *lookout* derives from this idiom.

- Their rear window *looks out on* a lovely garden.

- The soldiers watched for enemy troops from their *lookout* on the hill.

to stir up: to cause anger or strong emotion **(S)**; to create (trouble or difficulty) **(S)**

- The senseless murder of a small child *stirred up* the whole neighborhood.

- The boss is in a bad mood today so don't *stir* her *up* with any more customer complaints.

to take in: to visit in order to enjoy **(S)**; to decrease the size of clothes **(S)**; to deceive, to fool **(S)**

- We decided to *take in* Toronto on our trip to Canada, and that is where we *took in* the most memorable outdoor stage play we have ever seen.

- Lois lost so much weight that she had her skirts and slacks *taken in* by her tailor.

- The fraudulent investment advisor *took* everyone *in* with his sincere manner and generous promises. Most investors lost all their money.

EXERCISES

 A
Substitute an idiomatic expression for the word or words in italics, making any necessary grammatical changes as well. Then complete each sentence appropriately with your own idea. Also try to use idioms from previous lessons.

1. Many of the lakes in this part of the country have *lost all moisture* because . . .

2. When I asked Ted what he *was doing,* he responded that . . .

3. Karen hopes this meeting *stops* soon because . . .

4. If the government wants to *terminate* drug abuse in this country, it will have to . . .

5. Ruth *sought revenge on* the girl who stole her boyfriend away from her by . . .

6. Because our son Allen is always *joking,* nobody . . .

7. The house for sale was a valuable piece of property because it *faced* . . .

8. Old-time residents in the neighborhood became *angered* when their new neighbor . . .

9. Marge has lost so much weight in the last month that she has had to *decrease the size of* . . .

10. We visited the San Diego Zoo in order to *visit and enjoy* . . .

B *Answer these questions orally by making use of the idiomatic expressions studied in this lesson.*

1. When driving during rainy weather, why should you *slow down?*

2. Imagine that a country is facing a budget crisis. Which type of government funds are most likely to *dry up* first—those for social programs or those for military programs? Why? What is your opinion about the criteria used in such cases?

3. How might a person with a drinking problem be able to *dry out?* What kinds of problems might keep them from *sobering up?*

4. If someone asked you what you *were up to* these days, how would you respond?

5. How can you tell when young children *are up to something?* Can you remember any personal experience of *being up to something* when you were a child?

6. When might someone choose to *beat around the bush?* What could you do to avoid this?

7. What problems in the world would you like to *put an end to?* Do you think that there is hope for this?

8. Has someone ever *stirred you up* so much that you wanted to *get even with* him or her? What did you do?

9. What attractions in the area that you are living in now have you already *taken in?*

10. Have you ever been *taken in* by someone such as a salesperson or a stranger on the street? What happened?

Lesson 31

to go through: to undergo, to experience; to consume, to use (also: **to use up**)
The first definition is used when someone is having some hardship or difficulty.

- I can't believe what she *went through* to get that job. She had four interviews in one week!

- Frank said that they had *gone through* all the toilet paper in the house, but Steve couldn't believe that they had *used* it all *up*.

to go without saying: to be known without the need to mention
This idiom occurs with a *that*-clause, often with the pronoun *it* as the subject.

- It *goes without saying* that you shouldn't drive fast in bad weather.

- That he will gain weight if he continues to eat and drink so much *goes without saying*.

to put (someone) on: to mislead by joking or tricking **(S)**
This idiom is usually used in a continuous tense form. A noun object must divide the idiom.

- Don't worry. I wouldn't expect you do all that work by yourself. I'm just *putting* you *on*.

- Jack can't be serious about what he said. He must be *putting* us *on*.

to keep one's head: to remain calm during an emergency

- When the heater caused a fire, Gloria *kept her head* and phoned for assistance right away; otherwise, the whole house might have burned down.

- When the boat starting sinking in heavy seas, the crew members *kept their heads* and led the passengers to the lifeboats.

to lose one's head: not to think clearly, to lose one's self-control

- When a dog ran in front of Mel's car, he *lost his head* and drove onto the sidewalk and into a tree.

- If the politician hadn't gotten stirred up and *lost his head,* he never would have criticized his opponent unfairly.

narrow-minded: not willing to accept the ideas of others (the opposite of *narrow-minded* is **broad-minded** or **open-minded**)

- *Narrow-minded* people tend to discriminate against groups of people with which they have nothing in common.

- Ted is so *broad-minded* that he has almost no standards by which he judges others.

to stand up: to withstand use or wear; to fail to appear for a date or social engagement **(S)**

- My old car has *stood up* well over the years. I haven't had any major problems at all.

- Janet was very angry because her new boyfriend *stood* her *up* on their second date. She waited over an hour for him before returning home.

to get the better of: to win or defeat by gaining an advantage over someone

- Jim doesn't seem very athletic at tennis, but if you're not careful, he'll *get the better of* you.

- Lynn gets frustrated when Bruce *gets the better of* her in arguments. No matter what she says, he always has a clever response.

to break loose: to become free or loose, to escape

- During the bad storm, the boat *broke loose* from the landing and drifted out to sea.

- One bicyclist *broke loose* from the pack of racers and pulled ahead towards the finish line.

on edge: nervous, anxious; upset, irritable

- Cynthia was *on edge* all day about the important presentation she had to give to the local citizens group.

- I don't like being around Jake when he's *on edge* like that. Someone should tell him to calm down and relax.

to waste one's breath: to speak uselessy
This idiom is used when someone is wasting time trying to convince another person. The idiom **to save one's breath** is related and means *not to waste effort trying to convince someone.*

- Don't argue with Frank any longer. You *are wasting your breath* trying to get him to agree with you.

- I have already decided what I'm going to do. You can't change my mind, so *save your breath*.

to cut short: to make shorter, to interrupt **(S)**

- The moderator asked the speaker to *cut short* his talk because there wasn't much time remaining for questions from the audience.

- We were very unfortunate when we received bad news from home that forced us to *cut* our trip *short*.

EXERCISES

A

Substitute an idiomatic expression for the word or words in italics, making any necessary grammatical changes as well. Then complete each sentence appropriately with your own idea. Also try to use idioms from previous lessons.

1. Mr. Larsen is in the hospital *undergoing* emergency surgery because he . . .

2. When you feel sick, it *doesn't need to be mentioned* that . . .

3. Steve was *misleading me* when he told me that . . .

4. After the serious earthquake, most people *remained calm,* but unfortunately some people . . .

5. If a person is *not willing to accept the ideas of others,* you will probably *speak uselessly* if you try to . . .

6. Betty *failed to appear for* her date because she . . .

7. Your car will *withstand use* longer if you . . .

8. Our team was able to *win by gaining an advantage over* the other team because . . .

9. The politician was *nervous* before she . . .

10. The meeting was suddenly *interrupted* because . . .

B *Answer these questions orally by making use of the idiomatic expressions studied in this lesson.*

1. Do you *go through* money quickly? What is your biggest expense?

2. Have you ever *gone through* a medical operation? What was it?

3. Do you enjoy *putting* others *on,* or are you a rather serious person?

4. During an emergency, how can you *keep your head?*

5. In what kind of emergency might you be likely to *lose your head?*

6. Do you generally consider yourself to be a *broad-minded* person? In what ways might you be considered a *narrow-minded* person?

7. Which countries are known for manufacturing products that *stand up* well?

8. Have you ever *stood* anyone *up?* What were the circumstances of the situation that caused you to do so?

9. In what sport would an athlete try to *break loose* from an opponent?

10. Does talking in front of a large audience put you *on edge?* Why or why not?

Lesson 32

to step in: to become involved or concerned with something; to enter a place for a brief time
(also: **to step into**)

- When the children started fighting on the playground, a teacher had to *step in* and stop the fight.

- The supervisor asked one of the employees to *step into* her office for a moment.

to step down: to retire or leave a top position, to resign

- Next May the principal will *step down* after thirty-five years of service to the school.

- The angry shareholders wanted the company president to *step down* because of the stock scandal.

to step on it: to go faster, to work more quickly

- We're going to be late for the movies. You'd better *step on it!*

- If I want to finish this assignment by the end of the day, I really need to *step on it.*

a steal: very inexpensive, a bargain
This idiom is often used in an exclamation using *what.*

- I can't believe that I paid only $4,000 for this three-year-old car. What *a steal!*

- Scott considered it *a steal* when he bought a complete bedroom set for only $300.

to play up to: to behave so as to gain favor with someone (also: **to kiss up to**)

- The other students in the class resent Jim because he *plays up to* the teacher in order to get better grades.

- When my children asked me to go shopping for a new video game, I knew why they had been *kissing up to* me all morning.

more or less: approximately, almost; somewhat, to a certain degree

- Although your bedroom feels smaller, it's *more or less* the same size as mine.

- Ted *more or less* agreed with our decision to put off the meeting until more members could show up. At least he didn't object strongly.

to screw up: to confuse, to scramble **(S)**; to cause problems in or with **(S)**

- Chris had trouble finding Jane's apartment because the addresses of the buildings *screwed* him *up*.

- Instead of fixing the television set, the technician *screwed* it *up* even more.

to goof up: to perform badly, to make a mistake (also: **to mess up, to slip up**)

- I really *goofed up* on the exam today; did you mess up, too?

- Karen *slipped up* when she forgot to deposit money into her checking account.

to go off the deep end: to get very angry and do something hastily

- Just because you had a serious argument with your supervisor, you didn't have to *go off the deep end* and resign, did you?

- When Dan's wife demanded a divorce, he *went off the deep end* again. This time he was shouting so that the whole neighborhood could hear.

to lose one's touch: to fail at what one used to do well

- Milton used to be the best salesman at the car dealership, but recently he seems to have *lost his touch*.

● I used to play chess very well, but today you beat me easily. I must be *losing my touch*.

under control: well managed

● The police officer radioed to the station that she had the emergency situation *under control* and didn't need any assistance.

● Thank you for offering to help with dinner, but I think I have it *under control*.

to drag one's heels/feet: to act slowly or reluctantly

● My landlord is *dragging his heels* about fixing the furnace. If he doesn't fix it soon, I'm going to refuse to pay rent.

● Milla seemed willing to organize the volunteer activity, but now she is *dragging her feet*.

EXERCISES

 Substitute an idiomatic expression for the word or words in italics, making any necessary grammatical changes as well. Then complete each sentence appropriately with your own idea. Also try to use idioms from previous lessons.

1. During the lengthy workers' strike, the police had to *become involved* when . . .

2. After leaving his office down the hall, my supervisor *briefly entered* my office to . . .

3. The old man who founded the company decided to *retire* when . . .

4. Mike thought that the camera advertised in the newspaper was *a bargain,* so he . . .

5. The children *behaved so as to gain favor with* their parents in order to . . .

6. The young child *caused problems with* his bicycle by . . .

7. Lenny *performed badly* on the physics test because he . . .

8. I hope that my husband doesn't *get angry and do something hastily* when he . . .

9. The orchestra's lead violinist seems to be *failing at what she usually does well.* At the performance last night . . .

10. The mayor *acted reluctantly* when asked to explain . . .

B *Answer these questions orally by making use of the idiomatic expressions studied in this lesson.*

1. If someone was being attacked by a thief, would you *step in* and help the person? Why or why not?

2. For what reasons might a top executive of a company *step down* unexpectedly?

3. Why might you have to *step on it* in the morning? Does this happen often to you?

4. What was the last item you bought that you considered *a steal?* Where did you buy it?

5. Have you ever worked on something and *screwed* it *up?* How did you finally fix it?

6. Have you ever *goofed up* on an important test? Why did it happen?

7. Have you ever *gone off the deep end?* What happened?

8. For what reasons might an athlete *lose his or her touch* at a sport? Has this ever happened to you?

9. Have you ever had to get a difficult situation *under control?* What was the situation?

10. Have you ever *dragged your heels* when you were supposed to be responsible for something? Explain what you did, and why.

Lesson 33

to kick (something) around: to discuss informally (over a period of time) **(S)**
(also: **to toss around**)

- At first my friends were reluctant to consider my suggestion, but they finally were willing to *kick* it *around* for a while.

- Brian thought that we should *kick around* the idea of establishing a special fund for supporting needy members of the club.

on the ball: attentive, competent, alert

- Jim was the only one who caught that serious error in the accounting statements. He's really *on the ball*.

- Ella was certainly *on the ball* when she remembered to reconfirm our flight arrangements. All the rest of us would have forgotten.

to make up: to meet or fulfill a missed obligation at a later time **(S)**; to create, to invent (an idea) **(S)**; to apply cosmetics to **(S)**; to comprise, to be composed of
Note that all of the definitions are separable except the last one.

- The teacher allowed several students who missed the exam to *make* it *up* during the next class.

- The little boy *made up* a bad excuse for wearing his dirty shoes in the house, so his mother punished him.

- Iris was able to *make* her face *up* in half the normal time because she didn't use much *makeup*.

- Two separate bodies—the House of Representatives and the Senate—*make up* the Congress of the United States.

to make up with: to resolve differences with
This idiom is used for differences of opinion between friends and lovers.

- Gundula *made up with* her roommate after their serious misunderstanding about arrangements for the party.

- After the bad quarrel the two lovers kissed and *made up with* each other.

to pull together: to gather, to collect (information) **(S)**; to gain control of one's emotions **(S)**
A reflexive pronoun must be used for the second definition.

- The reporter *pulled together* information from several sources in preparing the newspaper article.

- Mr. Simpson was so frightened when he heard footsteps behind him on the lonely, dark street that it took several minutes to *pull himself together*.

to be looking up: to appear promising or optimistic, to be improving
This idiom is used in a continuous tense, very often with the subject *things*.

- The board chairman is glad to report that things *are looking up* for the company after several years of declining sales.

- Prospects for building that new library in the downtown area *are looking up*.

to kick the habit: to stop a bad habit

- Once a child becomes accustomed to chewing his nails, it's difficult to *kick the habit*.

- The doctor advised the heavy cigarette smoker that his heart had become damaged and that he should *kick the habit* right away.

to cover up: to conceal, to hide **(S)**
This idiom is used for events that are potentially embarrassing to one's reputation, as well as against the law. The noun **coverup** derives from this idiom.

- The office worker tried to *cover up* his crimes, but everyone found out that he had been stealing office supplies.

- The political *coverup* of the bribery scandal failed and was reported by all the major media.

to drop off: to fall asleep; to take to a certain location **(S)**; to decrease (for the third definition, also: **to fall off**)

- My mother *dropped off* during the boring television show; her head was nodding up and down.

- I don't mind *dropping* you *off* at the store on my way to work.

- Business has been *dropping off* rapidly recently, but fortunately it hasn't been *falling off* as quickly as for our competitors.

to turn over: to place upside down **(S)**; to flip, to turn upside down; to pass or give control to someone **(S)**

- The teacher asked the students to *turn* the answer sheet *over* and to write a short essay on the back.

- Don't forget to *turn over* the eggs, or they will burn.

- Mr. Collins has decided to *turn over* his jewelry store to his son at the end of the year.

to go through channels: to send a request through the normal way
This idiom can be used with the adjective proper.

- If you *go through the proper channels* in this company, it's sometimes impossible to get anything done quickly.

- The police told the mayor that even she had to *go through channels* in reporting the burglary of her house.

the last straw: the final event in a series of unacceptable actions

- When John asked to borrow money from me for the fourth time, it was *the last straw*. I finally told him that I couldn't lend him any more.

- I can't believe that my roommate left the door to our apartment unlocked again. It's *the last straw*; I'm moving out.

EXERCISES

A *Substitute an idiomatic expression for the word or words in italics, making any necessary grammatical changes as well. Then complete each sentence appropriately with your own idea. Also try to use idioms from previous lessons.*

1. When the committee members . . . , they decided to *discuss* the matter *informally* for a while.

2. In playing sports, you have to be *alert* if . . .

3. The child tried to *invent* an excuse when . . .

4. Lynn doesn't ever have to *apply cosmetics* to her face; she . . .

5. The two lovers *resolved differences with* each other after . . .

6. Even though I've . . . , things *appear promising* now.

7. Sales *had decreased* so much that the store was forced to . . .

8. You should *flip* the chicken in the oven because . . .

9. Old Mr. Jenkins *gave control* of his company to his associate when . . .

10. The office worker didn't think that . . . if he *sent a request through the normal way* because . . .

B *Answer these questions orally by making use of the idiomatic expressions studied in this lesson.*

1. What is the benefit of *kicking* an *idea* around instead of making an immediate decision?

2. What kind of excuses do people *make up* for being late to an important event? Have you ever done this?

3. Do you know how many states *made up* the original United States in 1776? How many states *make up* the United States now?

4. Have you ever *made up with* someone? How did you feel about *making up with* the person?

5. Where could you go to *pull together information for a research report?* Would you enjoy doing so, or not?

6. Have you ever succeeded in *kicking the habit* of cigarettes, smoking, drinking alcohol, or some other bad habit? How were you able to do it?

7. Have you ever had to *cover up* an embarrassing situation? Can you now explain what it was?

8. Why do students sometimes *drop off* while they're in class? Has this ever happened to you?

9. When someone manages to *kick* a bad *habit* there is an interesting expression, *to turn over a new leaf,* that applies. Can you imagine what this expression means?

10. Have you ever faced a situation which you would describe as *the last straw?* What happened?

Lesson 34

to get cold feet: to become unable or afraid to do something
This idiom is usually used in the case of an important or dangerous action.

- Karl was supposed to marry Elaine this weekend, but at the last moment he *got cold feet*.

- Only one of the rock climbers *got cold feet* when the group reached the base of the hundred-meter cliff.

to trade in: to receive credit for the value of an old item towards the purchase of a new item **(S)**
This idiom is used to form the noun **trade-in**.

- The car dealership offered me $1,000 for my old car if I *traded* it *in* for a new model.

- The appliance company was offering a $50 *trade-in* during the special promotion for its new line of refrigerators.

face-to-face: direct, personal; directly, personally (written without hyphens)
This idiom can be used both as an adjective (the first definition) and as an adverb (the second definition).

- The workers' representatives had a *face-to-face* meeting with management to resolve the salary issue.

- The stepmother and her teenage soon talked *face to face* about his troubles in school.

to be with (someone): to support, to back (also: **to go along with**); to understand or follow what someone is saying

- Although others thought that we shouldn't *go along with* Jerry, I told Jerry that I *was with* him on his proposal for reorganizing the staff.

- After turning left at the traffic light, go two blocks and turn right on Madison. After three more blocks, turn right again. *Are* you still *with* me?

to be with it: to be able to focus or concentrate on (also: **to get with it**)

To be with it in the negative has the same meaning as **to feel out of it**. The related form *to get with it* is used in commands.

- Jack's really *with it* today. I've never seen him play such good soccer.

- You've done only a small amount of work in two hours. You're not *with it* today, are you?

- It's no excuse to say that you *feel out of it*. We need everyone's help on this, so *get with it!*

to fall for: to fall in love quickly; to be fooled or tricked by

- Samantha and Derek never expected to *fall for* each other like they did, but they got married within two weeks of having met.

- The Masons wanted to believe their son, but unfortunately they had *fallen for* his lies too many times to be deceived once again.

it figures: it seems likely, reasonable, or typical

This idiom is either followed by a *that*-clause or by no other part of grammar.

- *It figures* that the children were willing to help with the yardwork only if they received a reward for doing so.

- When I told Evan that his secretary was unhappy about not getting a raise, he said that *it figured*.

to make (someone) tick: to motivate to behave or act in a certain way **(S)**

This idiom is used within a *what*-clause.

- If a salesperson knows what *makes* a customer *tick*, he will be able to sell a lot of merchandise.

- It's been impossible for us to figure out what *makes* our new boss *tick*. One moment she seems pleasant and then the next moment she's upset.

to cover for: to take someone's place temporarily, to substitute for; to protect someone by lying or deceiving

- Go ahead and take your coffee break. I'll *cover for* you until you return.

- The criminal made his wife *cover for* him when the police asked if the man had been home all day. She swore that he had been there.

to give (someone) a break: to provide a person with another opportunity or chance **(S)**; not to expect too much work from **(S)**; not to expect someone to believe **(S)** This idiom is always divided by a noun or pronoun, and it is often used in a command form. For the third definition, the pronoun *me* must be used. This definition used to express disbelief or disagreement and is considered impolite in formal settings.

- The driver pleaded with the police officer to *give* him *a break* and not issue him a ticket for speeding.

- When the students heard how much homework the teacher wanted them to do over the holiday, they begged, "*Give* us *a break*, Professor Doyle!"

- Oh, Jim, *give me a break!* That's a terrible excuse for being late.

to bow out: to stop doing as a regular activity, to remove oneself from a situation The related idiom **to want out** indicates that someone desires to bow out.

- She *bowed out* as the school's registrar after sixteen years of service.

- One of the two partners *wanted out* of the deal because they couldn't agree on the terms of the contract.

to stick it out: to remain in an unpleasant situation or keep doing an unpleasant activity, usually for a certain amount of time

- Maya wants to quit college, but she promised her parents that she would *stick it out* until the end of the year.

- You might hate jogging at first, but if you *stick it out* for a while you'll probably start to enjoy it.

EXERCISES

A *Substitute an idiomatic expression for the word or words in italics, making any necessary grammatical changes as well. Then complete each sentence appropriately with your own idea. Also try to use idioms from previous lessons.*

1. At the amusement center, Sean was about to . . . when he *became afraid to do it*.

2. Leanne talked to her supervisor *directly* about . . .

3. The politician asked his friends if they *supported* him on . . .

4. Ted *fell in love with* the actress as soon as . . .

5. When Mrs. Garcia told her husband that their son . . . , Mr. Garcia responded, *"That seems likely."*

6. I don't understand what *motivates* Diana *to behave that way;* she . . .

7. The boss *gave* his employee *another opportunity* when . . .

8. When the teacher told the students that . . . , the students said, *"Don't expect too much work from us!"*

9. One of the members of the committee *removed herself from the situation* because . . .

10. Even though Noel was unhappy with . . . , she decided to *stick it out* because . . .

B *Answer these questions orally by making use of the idiomatic expressions studied in this lesson.*

1. Have you ever been about to do something important or dangerous, and then *gotten cold feet?* What was it?
2. Besides a car, what items can be *traded in* for new purchases? Have you ever *traded* something *in?* What was it?
3. Why might a student need to have a *face-to-face* talk with a teacher?
4. For what reasons might you not *be with it?* Are you *with it* today? Why or why not?
5. Have you ever *fallen for* someone who was deceiving you? How did you feel? How did you resolve the situation?
6. It's sometimes difficult to figure out what *makes* certain kinds of people *tick.* What kinds of people are like this?
7. In general, who would you feel compelled to *cover for?* Have you ever had to do this?
8. If you were a judge, under what condition might you give someone who had committed a serious crime *a break?*
9. What unbelievable statement might someone make that would cause you to respond, *"Give me a break!"?*
10. Why might you choose to *bow out* of a situation?

Lesson 35

to rub it in: to tease or remind someone of something negative or embarrassing to him or her

- "Hey, Katya, remember when you fell down on the dance floor at Sylvia and Sam's wedding?"

  "Of course I remember. You don't have to *rub it in*."

- I finally beat Joshua at chess last Friday, so I've been *rubbing it in* since then.

to rub the wrong way: to cause to feel negative about oneself; to make a bad impression **(S)**
A noun or pronoun must separate this idiom.

- That salesman *rubbed* me *the wrong way*. He tried to convince me to buy a car that I didn't even like.

- The job applicant was qualified for the position, but her strange personality *rubbed* the interviewer *the wrong way*.

to get a rise out of: to provoke a response from
This idiom is usually used when someone is teased into responding in anger or annoyance.

- You can kid me all day about my mistake, but you won't *get a rise out of* me.

- I *got a rise out of* Malcolm when I teased him about his weight. Malcolm weighs over two-hundred and fifty pounds.

to hang around: to stay or remain where one is, to wait (also: **to stick around**)
This idiom is used when someone is waiting for something to happen or for someone to arrive.

- Todd had to *hang around* the house all day until the new furniture was finally delivered in the late afternoon.

- Why don't you *stick around* for a while and see if Sarah eventually shows up?

to pick up the tab: to pay the cost or bill

This idiom applies when someone pays for the cost of another person's meal, tickets, etc.

- The advertising manager is flying to Puerto Rico for a conference, and her firm is *picking up the tab*.

- The government *picked up the tab* for the visiting dignitary. It paid for all of the lodging and meals, as well as transportation, during his stay.

by the way: incidentally

This idiom is used when someone thinks of something further in the course of a conversation.

- Movies are my favorite form of entertainment. Oh, *by the way,* have you seen the new picture that's playing at the Bijou?

- Vera's been divorced for three years now. She told me, *by the way,* that she never plans to remarry.

to let slide: to neglect a duty (S); to ignore a situation (S)

- Terry knew that she should have paid the electric bill on time instead of *letting* it *slide*. Now the utility company has turned off her service.

- When he tried to get a rise out of me by mentioning my failure to receive a promotion at work, I just *let* it *slide*.

search me: I don't know (also: beats me)

This idiom is used informally, usually as a command form.

- When Mr. Nguyer asked his wife if she knew why the mail hadn't arrived she responded, *"Search me."*

- When I asked Derek why his girlfriend wasn't at the party yet, he said, *"Beats me. I expected her an hour ago."*

to get off one's chest: to express one's true feelings **(S)**
This idiom is used when someone has long waited to express themselves.

- Ellen felt a lot better when she finally talked to a counselor and *got* the problem *off her chest*.

- Faye hasn't shared her concern about her marriage with her husband yet. I think that she should *get* it *off her chest* soon.

to live it up: to spend money freely, to live luxuriously

- Kyle and Eric saved up money for two years so that they could travel to Europe and *live it up*.

- After receiving a large inheritance from a rich aunt, I was able to *live it up* for years.

to liven up: to energize, to make more active (also: **to pick up**) **(S)**

- The teacher occasionally took the class on field trips just to *liven* things *up* a bit.

- The animals in the zoo began to *liven up* when evening came and the temperatures dropped.

- Many people have to drink coffee every morning just to *pick* themselves *up*.

to have a say in: to share involvement in (also: **to have a voice in**)

- The new vice-president was promised that she would *have a say* in developing the company's international expansion.

- The students are trying to *have a voice* in college affairs by gaining representation on administrative committees.

EXERCISES

Substitute an idiomatic expression for the word or words in italics, making any necessary grammatical changes as well. Then complete each sentence appropriately with your own idea. Also try to use idioms from previous lessons.

1. My friend once embarrassed herself by . . . , so whenever I see her I have *to tease her about it.*

2. My older brother is always able to *provoke a response from* me when he . . .

3. Why don't you *stay here* for a while longer? We're still . . .

4. The director *paid the bill* for the meal when he invited . . .

5. At the restaurant, Benjamin . . . , which really caused his date *to feel negatively about him.*

6. I understand that Bill . . . because he *neglected his responsibilities* again and again.

7. In order to *express their true feelings about a problem,* some people . . .

8. On their honeymoon, the young couple *lived luxuriously* by . . .

9. In order to *energize* the party, the host and hostess . . .

10. The preferred candidate for the new position would not . . . until management agreed that she would *share involvement in* budget matters.

B *Answer these questions orally by making use of the idiomatic expressions studied in this lesson.*

1. When you were a child, did you ever do something foolish and have someone *rub it in* later? What was it?

2. What kind of person is it easy to *get a rise out of?* What kind is it difficult to *get a rise out of?* Which are you?

3. If someone is late in meeting you, about how long would you *stick around* before leaving? Has this happened to you recently?

4. When was the last time that you *picked up the tab* for someone? Has anyone *picked up the tab* for you recently?

5. Are you the kind of person who is likely to make an issue out of a serious problem, or rather to *let it slide?* Why?

6. Can you think of a reason why the expression *search me* is used to mean *I don't know?* (In other words, why is the verb *search* used in this way?)

7. Why do people sometimes hold problems inside instead of *getting them off their chests* right away? Which approach are you most likely to take?

8. Have you ever had a chance *to live it up?* Describe what you did.

9. What are some different ways of *livening up* an event such as a wedding?

10. In a democracy, how do citizens of a country *have a voice in* government affairs?

Lesson 36

out of the question: impossible, not feasible

- Stephen told Deborah that it was *out of the question* for her to borrow his new car.

- Don't expect me to do that again. It's absolutely *out of the question*.

to have to do with: to have some connection with or relationship to
This idiom is often used in the negative, as in the first example.

- Ralph insisted that he *had* nothing *to do with* breaking the window.

- What does your suggestion *have to do with* our problem?

to check in: to register at a hotel or motel; to leave or deposit for transporting or safekeeping **(S)**

- Courtney arrived in town at mid-day and promptly *checked in* at the Plaza Hotel.

- There were dozens of people at the airline counters waiting to *check* their bags *in* for their flights.

to check out: to pay the bill at a hotel or motel and then leave; to investigate, to examine **(S)**

- The latest you should *check out* of the hotel is noon.

- The police received a call from someone claiming to have witnessed a murder. The police sent two detectives to *check* the call *out* right away.

to take one at one's word: to accept what one says as true, to believe
(also: **to take one's word for it**)

- You should be careful about *taking her at her word*. She's been known to say one thing but to do another.

- When he offered to be responsible for the fund raiser, I *took his word for it*. Now he's saying that he's not available to do it.

to serve (the/one's) purpose: to be useful, to suit one's needs or requirements

- I don't have a screwdriver to open this, but I think that a knife *will serve the purpose.*

- Jane prefers working to studying, so it *served her purpose* to drop out of school and take that job.

to cop out: to avoid one's responsibility, to quit
This idiom is an informal version of the second definition *to back out* (Lesson 29). The noun form **copout** means *an excuse for avoiding responsibility.*

- Evelyn had agreed to help us with arrangements for the party, but she *copped out* at the last minute.

- I can't believe that Cindy offered such an explanation for failing to show up. What a poor *copout!*

to line up: to form a line; to arrange to have, to manage to obtain **(S)**

- The moviegoers *lined up* in front of the theater to see the most popular film of the summer.

- Rob is going to schedule the famous author to speak at the convention if he can *line her up* in time.

to lose one's cool: to get excited, angry, or flustered

- Despite the boos from some in the audience, the actors on stage never *lost their cool.*

- Although the group of skiers were in danger from an apparent avalanche, their ski guide never *lost his cool.*

to leave open: to delay making a decision on **(S)**

- In making up the job announcement, the firm decided to *leave* the salary *open* until a qualified candidate was found.

- We know that the annual summer camp will be held in August, but let's *leave* the exact dates *open* for now.

to miss the boat: to lose an opportunity, to fail in some undertaking

- The precious metals market was looking up several months ago, but unfortunately most investors *missed the boat.*

- Mr. Vlasic's new business went bankrupt within a short time. He really *missed the boat* by opening a tanning salon near the beach.

to think up: to invent, to create (also: **to dream up**)
This idiom is often used for an unusual or foolish thought.

- Who *thought up* the idea of painting the living room walls bright red?

- When asked by the teacher why she was late, the student *dreamed up* a plausible excuse.

EXERCISES

 Substitute an idiomatic expression for the word or words in italics, making any necessary grammatical changes as well. Then complete each sentence appropriately with your own idea. Also try to use idioms from previous lessons.

1. The Smiths *registered* at the hotel as soon as . . .

2. The Smiths also *deposited* some jewelry at the front desk because . . .

3. The jealous husband hired a private detective to *investigate* the possibility that . . .

4. When my financial advisor told . . . I *believed her.*

5. On the Thursday before a three-day holiday weekend, it *suited the worker's needs* to . . .

6. While shopping in the expensive store, Mrs. Thurston . . . *very much.*

7. To ensure . . . , the politician *managed to obtain* the support of his colleagues in the Senate.

8. The athlete *got angry and flustered* on national television when . . .

9. We *delayed making a decision on* the arrangements for the wedding because . . .

10. Even though I had urged my parents to . . . , my parents *lost an opportunity* when the stock market . . .

B *Answer these questions orally by making use of the idiomatic expressions studied in this lesson.*

1. What kind of items beside jewelry might a guest want to *check in* at the front desk of a hotel?

2. What is the latest that you have ever been able to *check out* of a hotel? Were you required to pay on extra fee for this arrangement?

3. If you and a friend are walking on a beach, what do you think your friend could mean if he or she says, *"Check that out!"*

4. Have you ever *taken someone at his or her word,* only to be disappointed at a later time? What happened?

5. Has anyone ever asked you for something that was *out of the question?* What did the person want?

6. Have you ever copped out of a responsibility by *thinking up* a reasonable excuse? How do you feel when you do this? Why?

7. Think of different kinds of events or situations where people have to *line up.*

8. What kind of situation might cause you to *lose your cool?* Does this happen easily to you, or not?

9. Why might you *leave* arrangements for a trip *open?* Has this ever happened to you?

10. What kind of activities do you want to *have* nothing *to do with?*

Lesson 37

to throw (someone) a curve: to introduce an unexpected topic, causing embarrassment **(S)**

- The first week of class was going very well until a student *threw* the teacher *a curve* by suggesting that the textbook was too difficult.

- The director asked us in advance to stick to the meeting agenda and not to *throw* him *any curves*.

to make waves: to create a disturbance, usually by complaining
This idiom is similar in meaning to the previous idiom, but the emphasis is on the aspect of complaining rather than causing embarrassment.

- In most companies, an employee who *makes waves* is not appreciated.

- The restaurant made many improvement after customers *made waves* about its poor food and customer service.

to carry on: to continue as before; to conduct, to engage in; to behave in an immature manner

- Even in the face of disaster, the inhabitants *carried on* as though nothing had happened.

- The business associates decided to *carry on* their discussion in the hotel bar instead of the conference room.

- I can't believe that John *carried on* so much just because his pet bird died. He looked depressed for weeks after it happened.

not on your life: absolutely not (also: **no way**)
This idiom is used as a kind of exclamation by itself.

- You're asking me to invest in that poorly rated company just because you know the son of the president? *Not on your life!*

- When a friend tried to get Mark to jump out of a plane with a parachute, he immediately responded, *"No way!"*

to cover ground: to be extensive, to discuss much material
Forms such as *a lot of, too much, too little* are used before the noun *ground.*

- The government's report on public schools *covers a lot of ground.* Many of the recommendations are too costly to implement.

- In his first lecture on Greek philosophers, I thought that our professor *covered too little ground.*

to throw the book at: to punish with full penalty, to be harsh on

- Because the criminal was a repeat offender, the judge *threw the book at* him with heavy fines and a long prison term.

- My boss *threw the book at* me when he discovered that I had been using company time for personal business. I was severely reprimanded and forced to make up the lost time.

to put one's foot in: to say or do the wrong thing
This idiom is used with the noun phrase *one's mouth,* when referring something said, or the pronoun *it,* when referring to something done.

- Fred really *put his foot in his mouth* when he called his supervisor by the wrong name.

- I really *put my foot in it* when I forgot my girlfriend's birthday and didn't buy her anything.

to be up for grabs: to become available to others
This idiom is used when something is highly desirable to many other people.

- When one of the full-time contract instructors stepped down, her nice office overlooking the river *was up for grabs.*

- Did you know that Senator Stone is retiring and that her Senate seat *is up for grabs?*

to show off: to display one's ability in order to attract attention **(S)**; to let others see, to expose to public view **(S)**
This idiom can form the noun **showoff** for the first definition.

- Elizabeth is an excellent swimmer, but I don't like the way she *shows off* in front of everyone. It's very obvious that she enjoys being a showoff.

- Jacquie *showed* her large engagement ring *off* to all her friends.

to learn the ropes: to become familiar with routine procedures
The related idiom **to show the ropes (S)** means to teach someone the routine procedures.

- The job applicant didn't have much previous experience or knowledge, but she seemed intelligent enough to *learn the ropes* quickly.

- It took the new schoolteacher a year to *learn the ropes* regarding administative and curricular matters.

- The new worker's colleagues helped to *show* her *the ropes*.

to have under one's belt: to have in one's experience, ownership, or accomplishments

- When Mr. Mott retired, he had 40 years of teaching *under his belt*.

- Fiona has several writing awards *under her belt*, even though she is still very young.

to keep one's fingers crossed: to hope to have good results, to hope that nothing bad will happen
This idiom reflects the way people cross their fingers to hope for good luck.

- Let's *keep our fingers crossed* that we got passing grades on that college entrance exam.

- Jerry *kept her fingers crossed* that the good weather would hold up for the picnic she was planning for the coming weekend.

EXERCISES

A *Substitute an idiomatic expression for the word or words in italics, making any necessary grammatical changes as well. Then complete each sentence appropriately with your own idea. Also try to use idioms from previous lessons.*

1. After discovering some improper contracts arranged by his company, a worker *created a disturbance by* . . .

2. The professor decided to *conduct* her class in the park because . . .

3. The teenager *behaved in an immature manner* for quite a while when his parents . . .

4. Martha answered, *"Absolutely not!"*, when her friend . . .

5. Because the instructor would *discuss too many matters* in the course, the student . . .

6. Maureen has a lot of work time *in her experience.* She . . .

7. The judge *was harsh on* the defendant who . . .

8. The long-time manager's office suddenly *became available to others,* and many associates . . .

9. The excellent athlete *displayed his ability and attracted attention* at the regional track meet by . . .

10. It was difficult for . . . *to become familiar with the routine procedures* at the university.

B *Answer these questions orally by making use of the idiomatic expressions studied in this lesson.*

1. Has anyone *thrown you a curve* recently? What happened?
2. When might a government worker decide to *make waves?* Have you heard or read of any instances of this recently?
3. Where is a common place to *carry on* a discussion? What less common places might a discussion be *carried on?*
4. Do you remember ever *carrying on* when you were a child? What did your parents do to stop you?
5. Do you like to take classes that *cover a lot of ground* or *cover little ground?* Why?
6. Would it ever be appropriate to *throw the book at* someone for *putting their foot in their mouth?* Why or why not?
7. Do you know anyone who likes to *show off?* What do they do?
8. Are you ever a *showoff?* When?
9. Have you ever had to *show* someone *the ropes* of a task they didn't know? What was the task?
10. Give an example of when you might *keep your fingers crossed.*

Lesson 38

to land on one's feet: to recover safely from an unpleasant or dangerous situation
(also: **to get back on one's feet**)

- After a series of personal and professional difficulties, it's amazing that George *has landed on his feet* so quickly.

- Some young adults get into so much trouble at school that they are never able to *get back on their feet* again. They drop out before graduating.

to dish out: to distribute in large quantity **(S)**; to speak of others in a
critical manner **(S)**

- Mary's mom *dished out* two or three scoops of ice cream for each child at the birthday party.

- Larry can't seem to take any criticism of his actions but he certainly likes to *dish* it *out*.

to get through to: to communicate with, to make someone understand (also: **to break through to**)

- Some of the students in my reading class understand English so poorly that it is difficult to *get through to* them.

- The doctors have never succeeded in *breaking through to* Mr. Ames, who is a silent and secretive patient.

to keep one's word: to fulfill a promise, to be responsible
An idiom with the opposite meaning is **to break one's word**.

- Suzanne *kept her word* to me not to let on to others that I intend to step down next month.

- Thomas always intends to *keep his word*, but invariably the end result is that he *breaks his word*. He just isn't capable of being a responsible person.

to be in over one's head: to be very busy, to have too much to do (also: **to be up to one's ears**); to be beyond one's ability to understand
For the second definition, the preposition *in* is not used.

- Huda is *in over her head* this semester. She is taking four classes, and she is *up to her ears* in assignments.

- It was impossible for the tutor to get through to Bill about the physics problem because the subject matter was *over Bill's head*.

to ask for: to deserve, to receive a just punishment (also: **to bring upon oneself**)

- If you drink alcohol and then drive a car, you're only *asking for* trouble.

- Don't complain about your cut in salary. You *asked for* it by refusing to heed our repeated warnings not to be late and inefficient.

to be a far cry from: to be very different from

- I enjoyed visiting Seattle, but it *was a far cry from* the ideal vacation spot I expected.

- Ned is enjoying his new job, but his responsibilities *are a far cry from* what he was told they would be.

by all means: certainly, definitely, naturally (also: **of course**)

- If the Johnsons invite us for dinner, then *by all means* we have to return the invitation. *Of course,* we don't have to invite their children, too.

to get out from under: to restore one's financial security, to resolve a difficult financial obligation

- After years of struggling to get ahead, the young couple finally *got out from under* their debts.

- The ailing company, succeeding in obtaining the necessary cash, was able *to get out from under* its financial burdens.

to take the bull by the horns: to handle a difficult situation with determination
This idiom is usually used when someone has been postponing an action for some time and finally wants or needs to resolve it.

- After three years of faithful service, Jake decided to *take the bull by the horns* and ask his boss for a raise.

- Vic has been going out with Laura for a long time now, and I know that he loves her. He should *take the bull by the horns* and ask her to marry him.

to give (someone) a hand: to assist, to aid, to help (also: **to lend someone a hand**) **(S)**

- Would you *give* me *a hand* lifting this heavy box?

- When Terry's car broke down at night on the highway, no one would stop to *lend* her *a hand*.

to give (someone) a big hand: to clap one's hands in applause, to applaud **(S)**

- After the talented new vocalist had sung her number, the audience *gave* her *a big hand*.

- Should we *give a big hand* to each performer as she is introduced, or should we wait until all the introductions are finished?

EXERCISES

 Substitute an idiomatic expression for the word or words in italics, making any necessary grammatical changes as well. Then complete each sentence appropriately with your own idea. Also try to use idioms from previous lessons.

1.   It took some time for the artist to *recover from the difficult situation* . . .

2.   Billy's mother *distributed in large quantity* . . . to all the kids at the birthday party.

3. When parents are having trouble *communicating with* their children, they can . . .

4. When I decided to change apartments, my friend *fulfilled her promise* about . . .

5. Larry *has too much to do* at work because . . .

6. The child running on the wet pavement beside the swimming pool *deserved it* when . . .

7. The new immigrant thought that . . . in the United States *was very different from* . . .

8. After days of postponing necessary yardwork, Mr. Johnson *handled the difficult situation* and . . .

9. When Kim's fell down on the icy sidewalk, a passing woman *assisted* her by . . .

10. The President *was applauded* when he announced . . .

B *Answer these questions orally by making use of the idiomatic expressions studied in this lesson.*

1. The idiom *to land on one's feet* is related to a special ability of cats. Do you know what this is?

2. Do you know anyone who doesn't like to receive criticism but is willing to *dish* it *out?* How do you feel about such a person?

3. Why is it often difficult *to get through to* young children? Is this sometimes true for adults? Why?

4. Is it always important for you to *keep your word?* Can you think of a situation where you would *break your word?*

5. Have you ever had a class where the subject matter *was over your head?* What did you do?

6. If you run across a street without looking first, you *are asking for trouble.* Try to think of other situations where you're *asking for trouble.*

7. What parts of an adult's life *are a far cry from* the life of a child?

8. If you see a beggar on the street is there anything that you do *by all means?*

9. Have you ever been forced to *take the bull by the horns?* What was the situation?

10. In what case might you refuse to *give someone a hand?*

Lesson 39

behind (one's) back: without one's knowledge, secretly
This idiom is used to describe acts of betrayal or dishonesty. It is often used with the verbs *to go* and *to talk*.

- After Carlo agreed to sell his car to me, he went *behind my back* and sold it to someone else instead.

- Bekah was angry when she discovered that her friends had been saying rude things about her *behind her back*.

to talk back to: to answer in a rude manner, to speak to disrespectfully

- Billy, if you *talk back to* me like that once more, you're going to spend the rest of the day in your room.

- The school principal had to reprimand the child for *talking back to* her teacher.

to be in: to be popular or fashionable; to be available at one's work or home

- Most young people tend to want anything that *is in* at the time, but a few don't care about current trends.

- Could you please tell me when Mrs. Zachary *will be in?* I'd like to talk to her soon.

to be out: to be unpopular or no longer in fashion; to be away from one's work or home

- These days, loose jeans are in and tight jeans *are out*.

- I'm sorry, Mr. Jensen *is out* at the moment. Could I take a message?

to draw the line at: to determine to be unacceptable, to refuse to consider

- I don't mind helping him with his homework, but I *draw the line at* writing a term paper for him.

- The conference organizers tried to accommodate the needs of the various groups, but they *drew the line at* extending the conference by two days.

to get out of line: to disobey or ignore normal procedures or rules
(also: **to step out of line**)

- When a child *gets out of line* in that teacher's class, she uses the old-fashioned method of making the child sit in the corner of the room.

- Any employee who *steps out of line* by coming to work in an unacceptable condition will be fired.

dry run: rehearsal, practice session

- The college president requested a *dry run* of the graduation ceremony in order to ensure that all aspects went smoothly.

- Before the manager presented the reorganizational plans to the board of directors, he did several *dry runs* of his presentation.

to play by ear: to play music that one has heard but never read **(S)**; to proceed without plan, to do spontaneously **(S)**
The pronoun *it* is often used with the second definition.

- That pianist can play most popular music *by ear.* She never needs to read sheet music.

- My husband wanted to plan our trip carefully, but I argued that it was more fun if we *played* it *by ear.*

to be in (someone's) shoes: to be in another person's position, to face the same situation as another person

- If I *were in your shoes,* I wouldn't take too many classes this semester.

- When his boss finds out about that accounting error, I wouldn't want to *be in his shoes.*

to keep after: to remind constantly, to nag

- Lynn always has *to keep after* her children about cleaning up their rooms and doing chores around the house.

- Yen is so forgetful that it's necessary to *keep after* him about every little thing.

to fix up: to repair or put back in good condition **(S)**; to arrange a date or an engagement for another person **(S)**

- Instead of buying an expensive new home, we decided to buy an older home and *fix* it *up* ourselves.

- Since my visiting friend didn't have a date for dinner, I *fixed* her *up* with a male friend of mine. They got along very well together.

to be had: to be victimized or cheated

- When the jeweler confirmed that the diamonds that the woman had purchased abroad were really fake, she exclaimed, *"I've been had!"*

- The angry customer complained about being overcharged at the store, asserting that this was the third time that he *had been had*.

EXERCISES

A *Substitute an idiomatic expression for the word or words in italics, making any necessary grammatical changes as well. Then complete each sentence appropriately with your own idea. Also try to use idioms from previous lessons.*

1. When Joey *spoke disrespectfully* to his mother, she . . .

2. When he learned that the owner *wasn't available,* the visiting salesperson . . .

3. Greg is willing to help his brother with some household chores, but he *refuses to consider* . . .

4. If you *disobey the rules* one more time, I will . . .

5. The theater group did a *rehearsal* of the play before . . .

6. Mrs. Dixson has the special ability *to play* music *she has heard but never read.* She doesn't have to . . .

7. I wouldn't want *to be in Ted's position.* The police have discovered that he . . .

8. Every day after school, Harriet's parents have *to nag* her to . . .

9. I decided to *arrange an engagement for* him because he . . .

10. When Nori discovered that . . . , he realized that he had *been cheated.*

B *Answer these questions orally by making use of the idiomatic expressions studied in this lesson.*

1. Have you ever done something *behind someone's back?* What did you do? Did you feel guilty about it?

2. When you were young, did you *talk back to* your parents? Why or why not?

3. Do you pay attention to whether clothing fashions *are in* or *out?* What is an advantage of not paying attention?

4. Suppose that your boss sometimes asks you to stay late at the office and do extra work for him. At what point would you *draw the line* and refuse?

5. What happens to an athlete who *gets out of line* during a sporting event such as baseball or international football ("soccer" in the United States)?

6. If you had to give a speech in class, would you do *a dry run?* Why or why not?

7. When you travel, do you like to plan your trip carefully or to *play* it *by ear?*

8. When you were young, what did your parents have to *keep after* you about? Did you ever learn to remember it, or do you still forget?

9. Have you ever *fixed* someone *up* with a date, or have you ever been *fixed up* with a date yourself? Can you imagine why the term *blind date* is sometimes used in such cases?

10. Have you ever *been had* by someone you just met, such as a store clerk or a stranger on the street? What happened?

Collocations

Idioms are expressions made up of words that take on new and different meanings when they are used in combination with one another. Collocations, on the other hand, are simply words that are traditionally used together by native English speakers, so that their combination becomes expected. Unlike idioms, the individual words in collocations retain their own meaning. Collocations can occur in a number of different patterns, including adjective + noun, verb + noun, verb + adverb, noun + verb, and noun + noun.

clear a space: move things to make room for something else

- Before you put those books down, let me *clear a space* for them on the desk.

clear (someone's) name: prove that a person is not guilty of something

- Marthe worked hard to *clear* her son's *name* after he was accused of cheating.

clear (something) with (someone): get formal permission for an action

- The ambassador *cleared* it *with* the State Department before announcing that he was leaving the country.

clear (one's) throat: cough in order to speak more clearly

- The speaker took a drink of water and *cleared her throat* before continuing.

keep quiet: avoid complaining, telling a secret, or causing problems

- We knew they were doing something wrong, but we *kept quiet*.

- The working conditions were awful, but we decided to *keep quiet* because we were afraid we'd lose our jobs.

keep (something) in mind: remember a fact or piece of information, especially because it might be useful in the future

- You need to be at the airport two hours early now—*keep* that *in mind* when you leave for London.

keep to the subject: talk or write only about the immediate topic

- I know you want to talk about vacation plans, but please *keep to the subject* while we figure out the answer to this other problem.

keep the change: don't give back any money that has been overpaid, perhaps as a tip, or because the amount is so small

- I bought a newspaper at the airport with my last Brazilian reals, so I told the seller to *keep the change.*

EXERCISES

Fill in the blanks to complete the collocations.

My brother has a friend who just can't keep —he's always talking. Sometimes he gets himself in trouble. He never keeps who might be listening, so sometimes he really says the wrong thing. Last night, for example, he said he was taking his girfriend to a hockey game, but he forgot to clear her. She was really mad—she hates hockey! He had to do some fast talking to clear and get her to stop being angry.

Also he has a hard time keeping keeping ; he'll be talking about one thing and then switch to another, and it's hard to follow him. Sometimes my brother will make little noises, like clearing clearing , just to get his friend's attention and make him stop. At dinner the other night, he just talked and talked, and the waiter was standing there, waiting for us to pay. Finally my brother just handed the waiter a handful of bills and told him to keep keep .

Review: Lessons 28 to 39

A *Match the idiom in the left column with the definition in the right column.*

_____	1. let alone	a. I don't know
_____	2. on the ball	b. certainly, definitely
_____	3. search me	c. nervous, irritable
_____	4. by the way	d. rehearsal, practice session
_____	5. out of the question	e. and certainly not
_____	6. by all means	f. incidentally
_____	7. more or less	g. impossible
_____	8. a steal	h. in general
_____	9. dry run	i. attentive, alert
_____	10. on the whole	j. directly, personally
_____	11. on edge	k. approximately, almost
_____	12. face-to-face	l. very inexpensive

B *In the space provided, mark whether each sentence is true (**T**) or false (**F**).*

1. _____ If you have *landed on your feet* after financial difficulties, things probably *are looking up* in your life.

2. _____ If you *go through channels* in submitting a complaint, you are probably *making waves* in your company.

3. _____ If someone asks why you did something and you can't *think up* a good reason, you might respond, *"Search me."*

4. _____ If you know someone who likes to *put* others *on,* you can usually *take* that person *at their word.*

5. _____ If the subject matter of an academic field often *is over your head*, you may not *be cut out for* that field.

6. _____ Parents might *go off the deep end* if they have *to wait up for* their child very late without knowing what he or she *is up to*.

7. _____ If you get a problem *off your chest*, you are *beating around the bush*.

8. _____ If you are able to *get through* to someone, you have *wasted your breath*.

9. _____ If you *are* not *with someone* while they are explaining something, you *are catching on*.

10. _____ You might *back out* of an activity that could cause you *to get cold feet* at the last minute.

11. _____ If you dislike *playing* something *by ear,* you will probably *leave* it *open*.

12. _____ If you are *learning the ropes,* it is possible that you might *goof up* once in a while.

C *Fill in each blank with the appropriate form of the idioms using **give** listed below. Some expressions come from Lessons 1 to 27.*

give and take	to give up	to give in
to give off	to give out	to give one a break
to give birth to	to give one a hand	to give one a big hand

1. Mrs. Johnson was very surprised when she _____ twin boys.

2. Because it was the first time that I had fooled around in class, I asked the teacher _____.

3. A successful marriage is mostly a matter of _____ between husband and wife.

4. This box is too heavy for me to lift alone. Could you _____?

5. The lecturer was so interesting that the audience _____ at the end of the talk.

6. The man stood on the street corner and _____ advertising flyers to the people passing by.

7. Could you please take this garbage outside? It _____ a very bad smell.

8. The army forces _____ when they discovered that they were surrounded by the enemy.

9. I usually don't _____ so easily, but this work is too hard for me to do.

D *Fill in each blank with the appropriate form of the idioms using **keep** listed below. Some expressions come from Lessons 1 to 27.*

to keep one's head	to keep with	to keep in touch with
to keep one's word	to keep often	to keep in mind
to keep track of	to keep away	to keep one's fingers crossed

1. In the emergency situation, Alex was able _____ and save the child from drowning in the ocean.

2. At the racetrack, none of the horses were able _____ the horse that was expected to win the race.

3. When we visited Disneyland, we had to be careful _____ our children in the large crowds of people.

4. You have _____ Tanya to return the books or she will forget time and again.

5. You should _____ when you make a promise or others will think poorly of you.

6. Even though you're moving to another city, we should _____ each other as much as possible.

7. While I was cooking with hot grease on the stove, I warned others _____ in order not to get burned.

8. When teaching beginning-level English students, it is important _____ that their range of vocabulary is quite limited.

9. The weather forecast is calling for cloudy skies tomorrow. We should _____ that it doesn't rain during the picnic.

E *Fill in each blank with the appropriate form of the idioms using go listed below. Some expressions come from Lessons 1 to 27.*

to go through to	to go off the deep end	to go without saying
touch and go	to go wrong	to go around
to go over	to go off	to go with

1. I was too tired to get up in the morning when my alarm clock
_____, so I turned it off and went back to sleep.

2. My presentation to the class _____ so well that the
students gave me a big hand.

3. The delicate operation was _____ for several hours, but
finally the surgeons were able to finish successfully.

4. We just went to the store an hour ago to buy more soda, and already
there isn't enough _____.

5. I can't understand how we _____ so much soda in such
a short time.

6. You can't _____ if you give Camille chocolates for her
birthday. Chocolate is by far her favorite food.

7. Paige has a terrible temper. When something upsets her, she
_____.

8. That you should stay home if you are very sick _____.

9. Do you think that this grey shirt _____ these beige pants?

DICTIONARY SKILLS

These pages will help you find word meanings and other useful information in your dictionary. *Note:* All dictionary entries are adapted from the *Longman Dictionary of American English,* New Edition (Pearson Longman, 2002).

Finding the Word You Want

The **entry words** (the words being defined) in a dictionary are in alphabetical order. This means that the word *apple* comes before the word *banana* because the letter *a* comes before the letter *b* in the alphabet.

EXERCISE A *Put these words in alphabetical order.*

1. dog tiger cat horse   *cat dog horse tiger*

2. pea broccoli onion beans   _____

3. pen book computer desk   _____

4. tea coffee soda milk   _____

5. train airplane car bus   _____

Some words start with the same letter or the same two or three letters. Alphabetize words like this by the first letter that is different. For example:

game **ga**rden **ga**te   **gla**d **gla**ss **glo**be

EXERCISE B *Put these words in alphabetical order.*

1. part pack pants park   *pack pants park part*

2. draw drag dream drive   _____

3. scroll scream screen scuba   _____

4. cheese child chalk cheap   _____

5. shout shut shot shoot   _____

Words are often listed in their **base form**. For example, if you can't find *safely* in your dictionary, look up *safe*.

EXERCISE C *Complete the chart.*

If you can't find . . .	Look up . . .
1. decided	*decide*
2. houses	
3. coolest	
4. beautifully	

Guide words are the words at the top of dictionary pages. One is on the left-hand page and one on the right-hand page. They tell you the first and last word on these two pages. For example, if you are looking for the word *leather,* and you see the guide words *lead* and *leave,* you know that *leather* is on one of those two pages.

Guide Word   Guide Word

lead   444   445   **leave**

where": Could you direct me to the station?"

lead² *n* **1** [singular] the position or situation of being in front of or better than everyone else in a race or competition: *Lewis is still in the lead.* | *Joyner has taken the lead.*

as someone or something else: *He knows a lot more than I do—he's way out of my league.*

leak¹ /lik/ *v* **1** [I, T] to let a liquid or gas in or out of a hole or crack: *Somebody's car must be leaking oil.* | *The roof's leaking!* **2** [I]

leap•frog /'lipfrag/ *n* [U]   a children's game in which someone bends over and someone else jumps over him/her –**leapfrog** *v* [I, T]

leap year /'. ./ *n* a year when February has 29 days instead of 28,

mentioning an advantage to show that a situation is not as bad as it seems: *Well, at least you got your money back.* **c)** said when you want to correct or change something you have just said: *His name is Jerry. At least, I think it is.* **d)** even if nothing

EXERCISE D *Read the guide words. Then circle all the words that would appear on those two pages.*

Guide Words	Words on the Pages
1. forced forget	(foreign) forgive (forget)
2. occur official	office occupy often
3. piece pin	pill pilot pig
4. root route	rouse routine rope

Understanding the Main Parts of a Dictionary Entry

Dictionary entries provide much more than just definitions. They provide a wealth of different kinds of information. Look at the entry below.

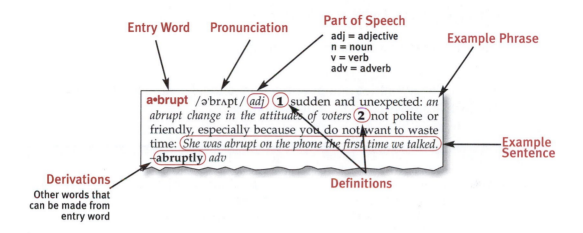

EXERCISE **A** *Use this dictionary entry to answer the questions.*

> **de•pressed** /dɪˈprɛst/ *adj* **1** very sad: *I got really depressed just thinking about her.* **2** not having enough jobs or business activity to make an area, industry etc. successful: *a depressed economy*

1. What is the entry word?   _____depressed_____

2. What is the part of speech?   _____

3. How many definitions are there?   _____

4. How many examples are there?   _____

5. Are there any derivations?   _____

Words often have more than one meaning. Read all of the definitions to find the meaning you need.

EXERCISE B *Which of the above meanings of* depressed, 1 *or* 2, *goes with each sentence? Circle 1 or 2.*

1. Business was **depressed** because of the war. 1 ②

2. I got **depressed** after failing my math test. 1 2

3. People can lose jobs in a **depressed** economy. 1 2

Read these dictionary entries and pay attention to the derivations. Notice that a part of speech is always given for a derivation.

in•ter•rupt /ˌɪntəˈrʌpt/ *v* **1** [I, T] to stop someone from speaking by suddenly saying or doing something: *I'm sorry, I didn't mean to interrupt you.* | *We'd only said a few words when Brian interrupted.* **2** [T] to stop a process or activity for a short time: *The war interrupted the supply of oil.* **–interruption** /ˌɪntəˈrʌpʃən/ *n* [C, U]

itch¹ /ɪtʃ/ *v* **1** [I, T] to have an unpleasant ITCH: *My back is itching.* **2 be itching to do sth** INFORMAL to want to do something very much: *Ian's been itching to try out his new bike.*

in•tim•i•date /ɪnˈtɪməˌdeɪt/ *v* **1** [T] to make someone afraid, often by using threats, so that s/he does what you want **–intimidation** /ɪnˌtɪməˈdeɪʃən/ *n* [U]

in•vis•i•ble /ɪnˈvɪzəbəl/ *adj* not able to be seen: *organisms that are invisible without using a miscroscope* **–invisibly** *adj* **–invisibility** /ɪnˌvɪzəˈbɪləti/ *n* [U]

EXERCISE C *Complete each sentence with the entry word or a derivative form of the word in parentheses. Use the information in the dictionary entries to help you decide.*

1. (interrupt) The _____interruption_____ didn't last long.

2. (itch) Her nose felt _____. She sneezed twice.

3. (itch) I have an _____ to go camping.

4. (intimidate) The government's _____ was wrong.

5. (intimidate) You can't _____ him.

6. (invisible) He tried to leave _____.

7. (invisible) The _____ of the glass was amazing.

Finding Collocations

Example phrases and sentences sometimes present collocations—words that are often used together. Read this dictionary entry. Pay attention to the example sentence.

> **fib**[1] /fɪb/ *n* INFORMAL a small, unimportant lie: *You shouldn't **tell fibs**. It's not nice.*

EXERCISE A *Circle the collacations in the example phrases and sentences in these entries.*

> **feud** /fyud/ *n* an angry quarrel between two people or groups that continues for a long time: *a bitter **feud between** the two neighbors* –**feud** *n* [I]

> **flee** /fli/ *v* **fled** /flɛd/, **fled, fleeing** [I, T] leave somewhere very quickly in order to escape from danger: *The president was forced to **flee the country** after the revolution.* | *thousands of people **fleeing from** the fighting*

EXERCISE B *Use the dictionary entries for* fib, feud, *and* flee *to help you complete these sentences with collocations.*

1. I wanted to _____flee from_____ the noisy room.

2. Linda says that her boyfriend is rich, but I don't believe her. She often

   _____.

3. Many people will _____ if a war starts.

4. There is a _____ those two soccer teams.

Finding Idioms

Idioms are common expressions with their own special meaning. For example, the idiom *have a green thumb* means "be good at making plants grow."

Many dictionaries present idioms in **bold type**. Sometimes they have their own definition number. Look at this example:

> **bread** /brɛd/ *n* [U] **1** a common food made from flour, water, and yeast: *We need a loaf of bread.* (=large piece of bread that can be cut into pieces) | *bread and butter* **2** SLANG money **3** sb's **bread and butter** INFORMAL where the owner of a business gets most of his/her·income from: *Tourists are our bread and butter.* **4** **daily bread** the money that you need in order to live **5** **know which side your bread is buttered on** INFORMAL to know who to be nice to in order to get advantages for yourself

EXERCISE A *Answer the questions.*

1. How many definitions are there for this entry word? _____

2. Write the numbers of the definitions that are idioms. _____

EXERCISE B *Read each idiom. Then write the word you would look up to find the idiom in a dictionary.*

1. head over heels in love _____head_____

2. make yourself at home _____

3. make your mouth water _____

4. a pat on the back _____

Using Phrasal Verbs

Phrasal verbs consist of a verb and an adverb such as *out, up, down,* and *up.* They have special meanings. Phrasal verbs are very common in English. To find a phrasal verb in the dictionary, look up the verb. For example, for the phrasal verb *dream up,* look under *dream.* In this entry, the phrasal verb is circled.

> **dream²** *v* **dreamed** or **dreamt** /drɛmt/, **dreamed** or **dreamt, dreaming 1** [I, T] to think about something that you would like to happen: *She* **dreamed about/of** *becoming a pilot.* **2** [I, T] to have a dream while you are asleep: *I often dream that I'm falling.* **3 dream on** SPOKEN said when you think that what someone is hoping for will not happen: *You really believe we'll win? Dream on!*
> **dream** sth ↔ **up** *phr v* [T] to think of a plan or idea, especially an unusual one: *Who (dreams up) these TV commercials?*

A dictionary such as the *Longman Dictionary of American English* tells you how to use a phrasal verb. Like other verbs, phrasal verbs can be **intransitive** or **transitive**. An intransitive phrasal verb cannot be followed by an object. Look at these examples:

set out: to leave on a trip

- They *set out* at 6:00 in the morning.

set aside: to save something for a special purpose

- We *set aside* some money for emergencies.

- We *set* some money *aside* for emergencies.

In these examples, *set out* does not have an object. It is an intransitive phrasal verb. *Set aside* has an object, *some money.* It is a transitive phrasal verb.

Notice that you can say **set aside** *some money* or **set** *some money* **aside.** When using most transitive phrasal verbs, you can put the object after the verb *(set)* or after the adverb *(aside).* But when the object is a pronoun, it must go after the verb: *We set it aside.*

In the dictionary, the objects of transitive phrasal verbs are shown as *sth* (something) or *sb* (somebody).

EXERCISE **A** *Study the dictionary entries for these phrasal verbs. Then choose the correct answer to the questions.*

set out *phr v* **1** set out to do sth to deliberately start doing something: *He set out to make a movie about his experiences in Vietnam.* **2** [I] to leave a place, especially to begin a trip: *The couple set out for Fresno at about 9:30.* **3** [T set out sth] to write or talk about ideas, rules etc. in a clear and organized way: *He is the first candidate to set out his foreign policy proposals.*

set sth ↔ **aside** *phr v* [T] **1** to save something for a special purpose: *Hotels must set aside 50% of their rooms for non-smokers.* **2** to decide not to be affected or influenced by a particular belief, idea etc.: *They should set politics aside and do what is best for the country.*

1. What tells you that you are looking at a phrasal verb?

   a. the abbreviation *sth*   b. the abbreviation *phr v*

2. What tells you that a phrasal verb is intransitive?

   a. [T]   b. *phr v*   c. [I]

3. What tells you that a phrasal verb is transitive?

   a. [T]   b. ↔   c. [I]

4. What tells you that a noun object can go in two positions?

   a. *phr v*   b. ↔   c. [T]

5. If you see this entry for a phrasal verb, which statement is true?

   come across sth *phr v* [T] **1** to discover something, usually by chance: *I came across the article in a magazine.*

   a. The object can go in two places.

   b. The object can go only after the adverb.

APPENDIX

ENGLISH	SPANISH	FRENCH	PORTUGUESE
Lesson 1			
get on	subirse, montarse	monter	entrar, pegar uma condução
get off	bajarse, apearse	descendre, sortir	descer de uma condução
put on	ponerse	mettre	por roupa, vestir, calçar
take off	quitarse	enlever	tirar, despir
turn on	encender, abrir	allumer, ouvrir	ligar, acender
turn off	apagar, cerrar	éteindre, fermer	desligar, apagar, fechar
right away	inmediatamente	immédiatement	imediatamente
pick up	tomar, coger	ramasser, prendre	apanhar, pegar, aprender
sooner or later	tarde o temprano	tôt ou tard	mais cedo ou mais tarde
get up	levantarse	se lever	levantar-se
come up with	proponer, sugerir	concocter, penser (à)	a princípio
at first	al principio	en premier, d'abord	achar, descobrir
Lesson 2			
dress up	emperifollarse, vestirse de gald	s'habiller, se mettre en grande toilette	vestir-se a rigor, com elegância
at last	por fin	enfin	finalmente, por fim
as usual	como de costumbre	comme d'habitude	como de costume
find out	averiguar	trouver, découvrir	descobrir
look at	mirar, contemplar	regarder, envisager	olhar para
look for	buscar, indagar	chercher, rechercher	procurar
all right	satisfactorio, afirmativo	c'est bien	está certo, tudo bem
all along	desde el principio	depuis le debut	o tempo todo, do começo ao fim

ENGLISH	SPANISH	FRENCH	PORTUGUESE
little by little	poco a poco, lentamente	au fur et à mesure	pouco a pouco, gradualmente
tire out	exhaustar, agotar	fatiguer	cansar, extenuar
spend time	pasar, dedicar tiempo	passer le temps à	gastar tempo
never mind	no se preocupe, no importa	peu importe, ne s'inquiéter pas	não se preocupe, não importa

Lesson 3

ENGLISH	SPANISH	FRENCH	PORTUGUESE
pick out	seleccionar, escoger	choisir	selecionar, escolher
take one's time	tomarse su tiempo, proceder con calma	prendre son temps	ir com calma, não se apressar
talk over	discutir	discuter	discutir (assunto)
lie down	acostarse	s'étendre	deitar-se
stand up	ponerse de pie	se mettre debout	levantar-se, ficar de pé
sit down	sentarse	s'asseoir	sentar-se
all day long	todo el día	toute la journée	o dia inteiro
by oneself	por sí mismo, solo	tout seul	sozinho, sem ajuda
on purpose	a propósito, adrede	exprès	de propósito, intencionalmente
get along (with)	llevarse bien o mal (con),	s'entendre, bien	dar-se bem
make a difference	ser importante, importarle	être important	importar, ter importância
take out	sacar, extraer	sortir	extrair, remover, sair na companhia

Lesson 4

ENGLISH	SPANISH	FRENCH	PORTUGUESE
take part in	tomar parte, participar	participer à	tomar parte, participar
at all	de ninguna manera, en absoluto	du tout	absolutamente, de modo algum
look up	indagar, buscar	chercher	procurar, pesquisar, consultar
wait on	despachar, servir	servir	servir, atender
at least	por lo menos	au moins	pelo menos, ao menos
so far	hasta ahora	jusqu'ici	até agora
take a walk	dar un paseo a pie, pasearse	faire une promenade	dar um passeio a pé, dar uma caminhada

ENGLISH	SPANISH	FRENCH	PORTUGUESE
take a trip	hacer un viaje	faire un voyage	viajar
try on	probar(se)	essayer	provar, experimentar (roupa)
think over	reflexionar	réfléchir	pensar, refletir
take place	suceder, ocurrir	avoir lieu, passer	acontecer, ocorrer, realizar-se
put away	guardar, recoger	ranger	guardar

Lesson 5

ENGLISH	SPANISH	FRENCH	PORTUGUESE
look out	tener cuidado	faire attention	ter cuidado
shake hands	dar la mano	serrer la main	dar um aperto de mão
get back	regresar	revenir, retourner	voltar, regressar
catch a cold	resfriarse, acatarrarse	prendre froid, attraper un rhume	pegar um resfriado, resfriar-se
get over	reponerse, restablecerse	se consoler, se remettre	recuperar-se, curar-se
make up one's mind	decidirse	se décider	decidir-se
change one's mind	cambiar de opinión o idea	changer d'idée, changer d'avis	mudar de idéia
for the time being	por ahora, mientras tanto	pour le moment	por enquanto, temporariamente
for good	para siempre, permanentemente	pour de bon	para sempre
call off	cancelar	annuler	cancelar, suspender
put off	posponer	ajourner	adiar
in a hurry	rápidamente	être pressé, rapidement	às pressas, com pressa

Lesson 6

ENGLISH	SPANISH	FRENCH	PORTUGUESE
hang out	vagar (por)	traîner	estar ocioso
hang up	colgar	suspendre, raccrocher (téléphone)	pendurar, desligar o telefone
count on	contar con	compter sur	contar com, confiar em
make friends	hacer amigos	faire des amis	fazer amigos
out of order	descompuesto, estropeado	en panne	enguiçado, quebrado

ENGLISH	SPANISH	FRENCH	PORTUGUESE
get to	llegar a	arriver à	conseguir, chegar
look over	revisar, examinar	examiner, vérifier	examinar, inspecionar
have time off	tener tiempo libre	avoir du temps libre	ter tempo livre
go on	continuar	continuer à	continuar
put out	sofocar, apagar, extinguir	éteindre	apagar (fogo)
all of a sudden	súbitamente, repentinamente, de pronto	tout à coup	de repente, subitamente
ahead of time	antes de tiempo, timprano	en avance	antes da hora, cedo

Lesson 7

point out	señalar, mostrar	signaler, montrer du doigt	mostrar, chamar atenção para
be up	terminar, llegar la hora	être terminé	terminar, expirar (tempo)
be over	haber terminado	être fini	estar terminado, terminar
on time	a la hora indicada	à l'heure, à temps	na hora, pontualmente
in time to	a tiempo, antes de la hora indicada	à temps	a tempo
get better	mejorar	aller mieux, s'améliorer	melhorar
get sick	enfermarse	tomber malade	ficar doente, adoecer
had better	es mejor que	il vaut mieux que	é melhor que
would rather	preferir	préférer	preferir
call it a day	parar de trabajar	finir la journée	dar por encerrado
figure out	resolver, entender	résoudre, comprendre	resolver, solucionar, entender
think of	opinar de	penser à	opinar, ter opinião sobre

Lesson 8

be about to	estar a punto de	être sur le point de	estar prestes a
turn around	dar la vuelta, cambiar totalmente	se retourner faire demi tous	virar ao contrário, dar a volta
take turns	alternar	alterner	alternar-se

ENGLISH	SPANISH	FRENCH	PORTUGUESE
pay attention	prestar atención	faire attention	prestar atenção
brush up on	refrescar, pulir	repasser	recordar (assunto), relembrar
over and over	repetidamente	sans cesse	repetidamente
wear out	gastarse	user	gastar-se, esgotar-se
throw away	botar, echar	jeter	jogar fora
fall in love	enamorarse	tomber amoureux	apaixonar-se
go out	cesar, apagarse, salir	sortir, cesser, s'eteindre	parar de funcionar, apagar-se, sair
go out with	salir con (alguien)	sortir avec (quelqu'un)	namorar
break up (with)	romper con	rompre avec	casamento, romper relaçöes com, terminar (um namoro)

Lesson 9

wake up	despertarse	s'éveiller, se réveiller	acordar
be in charge of	estar a cargo de	être chargé de	ser ou estar encarregado de
as soon as	tan pronto como	aussitôt que	assim que, logo que
have a good time	divertirse	bien s'amuser	divertir-se
in no time	rápidamente	tout de suite	num instante, rapidamente
cut down on	reducir	reduire	reduzir, diminuir
crack down on	actuar con dureza	sévir avec	ser exigente com, dar duro em
quite a few	muchos	pas mal de	muitos, vários
used to	acostumbraba, solía	avoir l'habitude de	costumava acontecer, era
be used to	estar acostumbrado a	être accoutumé à, avoir l'habitude de	estar acostumado a (fazer) algo
get used to	acostumbrarse a	s'accoutumer à prenare l'habitude	acostumar-se a (fazer) algo
back and forth	de un lado a otro	d'avant en arrière	de um lado para outro, para trás e para frente

ENGLISH	SPANISH	FRENCH	PORTUGUESE

Lesson 10

make sure	asegurar, garantizar	s'assurer de	verificar, certificar-se de
now and then	de vez en cuando	de temps en temps	de vez em quando
get rid of	deshacerse de	se défaire de, se débarasser de	desfazer-se de, livrar-se de
every other	cada dos	tous les deux	um sim um não, alternado
go with/ go together	armonizar con, acompañar	aller avec	ir bem com, combinar com
first-rate	primera clase, excelente	de première classe	de primeira ordem, excelente
come from	proceder de, ser oriundo de	venir de (quelque part)	vir de, proceder de, descender de
make good time	viajar rápidamente	voyager vite, bien marcher (train)	viajar depressa, dirigir em velocidade
mix up	equivocar, mezclar, confundir	mélanger, s'embrouiller, confondre	misturar bem, confundir, atrapalhar
see about	ocuparse de	s'occuper de	averiguar, examinar, pensar em
by heart	de memoria	par coeur	de cor, de memória
make an impression	causar impression	impressionner	dar a impressão de, influenciar a opinião de uma outra pessoa

Lesson 11

keep out	no entrar	défense d'entrer	não entrar
keep away	mantener distancia de, evitar	éviter	afastar, manter afastado
find fault with	criticar	trouver à redire	criticar, desaprovar
be up to	depender de alguien, tener entre manos	dépendre de	caber a, estar em condições de, ser capaz de
ill at ease	incómodo	mal à l'aise, peu confortable	constrangido, pouco à vontade
do over	volver a hacer	refaire	refazer, repetir
look into	investigar	examiner attentivement	investigar, examinar

ENGLISH	SPANISH	FRENCH	PORTUGUESE
take hold of	agarrarse de	saisir	agarrar-se, segurar, pegar
get through	terminar, acabar	terminer	terminar, acabar
from now on	de ahora en adelante	a partir de ce moment	de agora em diante
keep track of	llevar cuenta de	enregistrer, tenir un registre	acompanhar o desenvolvimento ou o curso de
get carried away	dejarse llevar, excederse	se laisser emporter	entusiasmar-se, empolgar-se

Lesson 12

up to date	moderno, al día, al corriente	au courant, à la page	moderno, atual
out of date	anticuado, antiquo, arcaico	démodé, périmé, dépassé	antiquado, obsoleto, fora de moda
blow up	inflar, explotar, volar	gonfler, faire sauter, exploser	encher de ar, explodir
catch fire	incendiarse	prendre feu	pegar fogo, incendiar-se
burn down	quemarse (un edificio)	détruire par le feu	queimar lentamente, destruir pelo fogo
burn up	quemar (se) completamente, enojarse	brûler entièrement, se fâcher	destruir pelo fogo, indignar, aborrecer
burn out	fundirse	brûler	deixar de funcionar por muito uso, cansar-se
stands to reason	ser natural, lógico	il va sans dire	ser lógico, ser evidente
break out	estallar, comenzar súbitamente	éclater	surgir, manifestar-se
as for	en cuanto a	quant à, en tant que	quanto a, no que diz respeito a
for one thing	por ejemplo	par exemple	por exemplo
feel sorry for	tener lástima de	avoir de la peine pour	ter pena de

Lesson 13

break down	romperse	tomber en panne	quebrar, avariar-se
turn out	resultar, acudir	finalement devenir, se presenter	reportar-se, apresentar-se, tornar-se

ENGLISH	SPANISH	FRENCH	PORTUGUESE
once in a blue moon	rara vez	une fois par hasard	raramente, uma vez ou outra
give up	dejar de, rendirse	se rendre, abdiquer, abandonner	desistir, parar, abandonar
cross out	tachar	barrer	riscar, cancelar, eliminar
take for granted	presumir, tomar por descontado	présumer, tenir pour certain	tomar como certo, não dar valor a algo
take into account	tomar en cuenta, tener en consideración	tenir compte de	levar em conta ou em consideração
make clear	aclarar	clarifier	explicar, esclarecer
clear cut	bien claro	net	bem definido, distinto, claro
have on	tener puesto, llevar	porter	vestir, trajar
come to	volver en sí ascender, llegar a	revenir à soi	voltar a si, recolher os sentidos
call for	requerir, recomendar	nécessiter, recommander	requerer, exigir

Lesson 14

eat in / eat out	comer en casa/ comer fuera	manger à la maison/ manger au restaurant	comer em casa/comer fora
cut and dried	predecible	simple, clair et net	previsível, sem graça
look after	cuidar de	s'occuper de	cuidar de, supervisionar
feel like	tener ganas de	avoir envie de	estar disposto a, estar a fim de
once and for all	de una vez y para siempre	une fois pour toutes	de uma vez por todas
hear from	recibir noticias de	recevoir des nouvelles	ter notícias de alguém
hear of	oír hablar de, saber de, considerar	entendre parler de, considérer	ouvir falar, considerar
make fun of	burlarse de	se moquer de, se rire de	ridicularizar, fazer gozação de
come true	resultar cierto	passer à la réalité	tornar-se realidade, realizar-se
as a matter of fact	en realidad, es más	le fait est que	na verdade, aliás

ENGLISH	SPANISH	FRENCH	PORTUGUESE
have one's way	salirse con la suya	en faire à sa tête, suivre sa volonté	conseguir fazer o que quer, impor a sua vontade
look forward to	aguardar con ansia	avoir hâte de impatience	aguardar ansiosamente, estar ansioso para fazer algo

Lesson 15

inside out	al revés	à l'envers	do avesso
upside down	boca abajo	sens dessus	de cabeça para baixo
fill in	rellenar espacio(s), informer	remplir, informer	preencher espaços
fill out	completar una planilla	remplir	completar um formulário, um cupom
take advantage of	aprovecharse de	profiter de	tirar proveito de, aproveitar-se de
no matter	no importa	peu importe	não importa (como), de qualquer modo começar a estudar
take up	estudiar, ocupar	étudier, occuper	ocupar (posição), tomar (tempo, espaço)
take up with	consultar con	discuter avec	consultar alguém
take after	salir a	tenir de	parecer-se com
in the long run	a la larga	à la longue	com o decorrer do tempo
in touch	en comunicación	rester en contact	manter contato com
out of touch	sin comunicación, desligado	avoir perdu le contact avec	não estar a par de

Lesson 16

on one's toes	alerta	alerte	estar alerta
watch one's step	andar/ir con cuidado	se surveiller, faire attention	andar com cuidado, tomar cuidado
watch what one says/does	tener cuidado con lo que uno hace/dice	faire attention à ce qu'on fait/dit	ter cuidado com o que fala ou faz
see eye to eye	estar de acuerdo	être d'accord sur tous les points	concordar plenamente, estar de acordo
have in mind	tener en mente, proponerse	avoir quelque chose à l'esprit	ter intenção de, pretender

ENGLISH	SPANISH	FRENCH	PORTUGUESE
keep in mind	recordar	se rappeler que	lembrar, não esquecer
for once	al fin, sólo una vez	pour une fois	por esta vez
go off	disparar, explotar, partir	exploser partir, s'en aller, sonner	explodir, ir-se embora
grow out of	quitársele, dar origen	passer	superar, amadurecer
make the best of	sacar el mejor partido posible	tirer le meilleur parti de	tirar o melhor proveito de
cut off	cortar	couper, interrompre	cortar, parar subitamente
cut out	recortar, cesar	découper, cesser de	recortar, parar de fazer algo

Lesson 17

ENGLISH	SPANISH	FRENCH	PORTUGUESE
blow out	reventarse, apagar (soplando)	avoir une crevaison, éteindre, souffler	explodir, estourar, apagar-se
become of	hacerse de, sucederle	devenir	acontecer
shut up	(en)cerrar/acorralar callarse	enfermer, mettre les verrous, se taire	fechar, calar-se
have got	tener, poseer	avoir	ter, possuir
have got to (do something)	tener que (hacer algo)	devoir	ter de
keep up with	mantenerse a la par de	aller aussi vite que	não ficar atrás, acompanhar (passo, progresso, etc.)
on the other hand	sin embargo	d'autre part	por outro lado
turn down	bajar, reducir, rechazar	baisser, refuser	abaixar, diminuir (som, luz, gás), recusar, rejeitar
fifty-fifty	a la mitad	moitié-moitié	meio a meio, em partes iguais
break in	estrenar, ajustar, interrumpir	assouplir, interrompre	amaciar, interromper
lost cause	causa perdida, inútil	une cause sans espoir	uma causa perdida
above all	sobre todo	par-dessus tout	acima de tudo, antes de mais nada

Lesson 18

ENGLISH	SPANISH	FRENCH	PORTUGUESE
do without	prescindir de	se passer de	passar sem, ficar sem
according to	de acuerdo con, según	selon	de acorddo com, segundo

ENGLISH	SPANISH	FRENCH	PORTUGUESE
be bound to	ser inevitable	être certain de	ser muito provável
for sure	con seguridad	vraiment	ao certo, com toda certeza
take for	tomar a uno por	prendre quelqu'un pour	tomar por, confundir com
try out	probar	essayer	testar algo, submeter-se a teste
tear down	derribar, demoler	démolir	demolir, derrubar
tear up	rasgar, lacerar	déchirer	rasgar
go over (well)	ser apreciado	passer bien	ter muito êxito, ter sucesso
run out of	acabarse, agortarse	manquer de	ficar sem ou em falta de
at heart	fundamentalmente	au fond	no fundo, na realidade
on hand	a la mano, disponible	à main, disponible	a mão, disponível

Lesson 19

ENGLISH	SPANISH	FRENCH	PORTUGUESE
bite off	aceptar una responsabilidad excesiva	viser trop haut	querer abarcar o mundo com as pernas
tell apart	distinguir entre	distinguer entre	diferenciar, distinguir
all in all	teniendo todo en consideración	tous comptes faits	no todo, em conjunto
pass out	distribuir, repartir, desmayarse	répartir, perdre conscience	distribuir, desmaiar
go around	alcanzar para todos, circular	suffire à tout le monde, circuler	dar ou ser suficiente para todos, circular, andar
be in the/one's way	estorbar	être de trop	no caminho, atrapalhar
put on	ganar peso, representar	augmenter de poids, réprésenter	ganhar peso, encenar
put up	construir, edificar levantar	construire, ériger, lever	construir, levantar, afixar
put up with	tolerar, soportar	tolérer, supporter	agüentar, tolerar
in vain	en vano	en vain	em vão
day in and day out	a diario, día tras día	bon an, mal an	dia após dia, diariamente
catch up	alcanzar	se rattraper	alcançar, pôr em dia

Lesson 20

ENGLISH	SPANISH	FRENCH	PORTUGUESE
hold still	estarse quieto	rester tranquille	ficar quieto, parado
break the news	dar la noticia	annoncer la nouvelle	dar a notícia (geralmente uma notícia ruim)
be the matter	pasar algo	avoir quelque chose de mal	haver de errado
bring up	criar, presentar	élever	criar, educar, mencionar
get lost	perderse	se perdre	perder-se, sumir
hold up	durar, demorar	durer, retarder	atrasar, reter
run away	huir, escaparse	se sauver, s'échapper	escapar, fugir
rule out	descartar	éliminer, renoncer à	excluir, descartar, não considerar
by far	claramente	de loin, de beaucoup	decididamente, sem comparação
see off	despedirse de alguien	voir partir quelqu'un	despedir-se
see out	acompañar a la salida	raccompagner à la porte	acompanhar alguém até a saída
no wonder	no extrañar	n'avoir rien d'étonnant	não admira, não há que se estranhar

Lesson 21

ENGLISH	SPANISH	FRENCH	PORTUGUESE
go up	ir hasta, llegar hasta	conduire à, aller à, courir à	subir, aumentar, erguer (prédios)
go up to	dirigirse a, acercarse a	s'approcher de	aproximar-se, dirigir-se a
hand in	presentar, entregar	remettre, donner	entregar
in case	por si acaso	au cas où	caso, se, no caso de
take apart	desarmar	démonter	desmontar, desarmar
put together	armar	assembler	montar, armar
be better off	irle mejor	valoir mieux	estar em melhores circunstâncias ou em melhor situação
be well-off	ser acomodado, tener dinero	être dans l'aisance	ter dinheiro, ser rico
take by surprise	sorprender a alguien	prendre au dépourvu	pegar de surpresa, pegar desprevenido

ENGLISH	SPANISH	FRENCH	PORTUGUESE
stress out	estresar, preocupar	stresser, inquiéter	estressar, preocupar
name after	darle el nombre de	être nommé d'après	dar o nome de alguém
hold on	agarrarse de, aguantar	s'accrocher à, attendre	agarrar, esperar

Lesson 22

stop by	visitar	s'arrêter en passant	dar uma passada
drop (someone) a line	escribirle unas líneas a alguien	écrire un mot	escrever umas linhas
give (someone) a call	llamar por teléfono	donner un coup de fil, téléphoner	ligar, telefonar
come across	encontrarse con, dar la impresión	trouver par hasard	encontrar, achar por acaso
cross one's mind	ocurrírsele a uno	(se) venir à l'esprit	passar pela cabeça de alguém
stand for	representar, aguantar a, tolerar	réprésenter, tolérer	representar, significar, tolerar
stand a chance	tener probabilidad	avoir la chance de	ter uma probabilidade
look on	observar	regarder	observar, ser espectador
look up to	admirar	avoir un grand respect pour	admirar, respeitar
look down on	despreciar	regarder de haut en bas	desprezar, tratar com superioridade
take off	despegar	décoller	decolar, partir
pull off	lograr, detener el coche en la carretera	réussir, arrêter l'auto	realizar, encostar o carro na margem da estrada

Lesson 23

make do	improvisar	faire, se débrouiller (avec)	arranjar-se, virar-se (com algo)
give birth to	dar a luz	donner naissance à, mettre au monde	dar à luz
close call	librarse por los pelos	l'échapper belle, passer à deux doigts de quelque chose	ato de livrar-se por um triz
get on one's nerves	ponerlo a uno nervioso	porter sur les nerfs	irritar, dar nos nervos

ENGLISH	SPANISH	FRENCH	PORTUGUESE
put down	dominar, reprimir, criticar injustamente	réprimer, critiquer injustement	reprimir, debeelar, humilhar
go for	venderse por (precio), aspirar a	se vendre à, essayer d'obtenir	valer, procurar conseguir, concordar
be into	ser aficionado a	s'adonner à s'intéresser a	ter interesse em, adorar fazer algo
stay up	acostarse tarde	veiller	ficar acordado
stay in	quedarse en casa	rester à la maison	ficar em casa
take over	encargarse de tomar or hacer otra vez	se charger de faire, prendre de nouveau	assumir a direção, o controle, fazer de novo
show up	presentarse, aparecerse, ser hallado	se présenter, être trouvé	aparecer, comparecer, ser localizado
clean out	limpiar	nettoyer (à fond)	esvaziar, limpar, tirar todo o dinheiro de

Lesson 24

knock out	hacer perder el sentido de un golpe	faire perdre connaissance par un coup	pôr alguém nocaute
knock oneself out	matarse del esfuerzo	se défoncer, se crever pour	matar-se de trabalhar, dar duro
carry out	llevar a cabo	exécuter	realizar, cumprir, pôr em prática
run into	encontrarse con	rencontrer par hasard	encontrar-se com, colidir
set out	solir a, exponer	se mettre en chemin	partir, sair, expor
set out to	emprender	se mettre à	propor-se a fazer algo
draw up	trazar, preparar	tracer, préparer	lavrar um contrato
give and take	hacer concesiones	s'accommoder, négocier	fazer concessões, toma-lá-dá-cá
drop out of	dejar de asistir	quitter	abandonar, desistir
believe in	creer en	croire à	acreditar em algo
cheer up	alegrarse, animarse	prendre courage, se réjouir	animar-se
make sense	ser razonable, tener sentido	être logique	fazer sentido, ser razoável

ENGLISH	SPANISH	FRENCH	PORTUGUESE

Lesson 25

ENGLISH	SPANISH	FRENCH	PORTUGUESE
burst out crying/ laughing	romper a llorar, echar a reir	fondre en larmes, éclater de rire	sair rapidamente, desatar a chorar ou a rir
get away	escapar, huir	s'échapper, s'enfuir	ir-se embora, escapar
get away with	salirse con la suya	s'en tirer	consequir fazer algo impunemente
serve (someone) right	merecer	mériter	ser bem feito, ser merecido
keep up	impedir el sueño, mantener el mismo paso	empêcher de dormir, continuer au même pas	não deixar dormir, manter, conservar
keep up with	estar al día, entender	être au courant, suivre	acompanhar (progresso), entender
stand out	sobresalir	se distinguer	sobressair, destacar-se
let on	dejar entrever, revelar	reveler à	dar com a língua nos dentes, contar (segredo)
go wrong	salir mal	marcher mal, ne pas marcher	dar errado, falhar
meet (someone) halfway	llegar a un acuerdo	faire des concessions	fazer concessões, entrar em acordo
check up on	revisar, comprobar	vérifier, examiner	investigar, verificar
stick up	sobresalir	ressortir	estar espetado (cabelo), assaltar

Lesson 26

ENGLISH	SPANISH	FRENCH	PORTUGUESE
come about	suceder, ocurrir	se produire	surgir, acontecer
bring about	causar, provocar	causer, provoquer	provocar, acarretar
build up	aumentar	se fortifier, renforcer	aumentar, desenvolver
die down	acabarse, apagarse	se calmer, s'éteindre	acalmar (tempestade, vento), diminuir, baixar (fogo, chamas)
fade away	desaparecer poco a poco	disparaître peu à peu	desaparecer gradualmente
die out	desaparecer	disparaître	desaparecer, extinguir-se
make out	descifrar, entender escribir	déchiffrer, écrire	compreender, decifrar, redigir (documentos), preencher (cheques)

ENGLISH	SPANISH	FRENCH	PORTUGUESE
live up to	cumplir, realizar	être à la hauteur de	cumprir (promessa)
stick to	defender, mantener firme	persévérer s'en tenirà	manter, sustentar, seguir com algo
rip off	robar alguien (cobrar demasiado), robo	voler, arnaquer, filouter, escroquerie	roubar alguém (cobrando demais), roubo (em preço)
stand up for	salir en defensa de	défendre	exigir, defender, apoiar
cut corners	economizar	réduire les dépenses	economizar

Lesson 27

take on	emplear, responsabilizarse	employer, engager	empregar, encarregar-se de
take down	descolgar, bajar, tomar nota de	décrocher, prendre note de	tirar, descer, escrever, tomar nota
fall through	fracasar	échouer	falhar, fracassar, dar em nada
fall behind	atrasarse	prendre du retard, être en arrière	ficar para trás, atrasar (pagamentos)
give in	darse por vencido, rendirse	se rendre à, céder	render-se, ceder
give off	producir, despedir	produire, exhaler	emitir, desprender (vapores)
give out	repartir, acabarse	distribuer, être épuisé	distribuir, esgotar-se, acabar
have it in for	tenérselas juradas a uno, tenerla cogida con uno	en vouloir à quelqu'un	quardar rancor, ter raiva
have it out with	poner las cosas en claro, ventilar un asunto con alguien	régler quelque chose	tirar a limpo, pôr tudo às claras
hold off	aguantar, aplazar	cesser, s'arrêter, retenir, retarder	atrasar, demorar
hold out	durar, ser suficiente, resistir	durer, être suffisant, résister	resistir, durar
hold over	mantener, posponer	continuer à montrer	manter, adiar

Lesson 28

let up	disminuir, aflojar, relajar	diminuer, relâcher	diminuir, relaxar

ENGLISH	SPANISH	FRENCH	PORTUGUESE
lay off	parar, dejar cesante, despedir	arrêter, mettre au chômage	abster-se, reduzir, dispensar empregados
bring out	sacar, presentar	présenter, faire paraître	mostrar, apresentar
bring back	devolver	rapporter	devolver, trazer de volta
wait up for	esperar por, desvelarse en espera de	attendre	ficar acordado esperando alguém
leave alone	dejar tranquilo	laisser tranquille	deixar em paz
let alone	sin mencionar	encore moins	quanto menos, quanto mais
break off	terminar, finalizar	rompre les relations avec	terminar, cortar relações
wear off	pasar, desaparecer	disparaître (peu à peu), s'user	passar (efeito, dor, etc.), diminuir gradualmente
wear down	gastar	user complètement	gastar, corroer
on the whole	en general	en somme, à tout prendre	de uma maneira geral
touch and go	arriesgado	risqué, incertain	arriscado, incerto

Lesson 29

work out	hacer ejercicio, planear, resultar	s'exercer, élaborer	malhar, treinar, planejar, resultar
back up	dar marcha atrás, defender	faire marche arrière, défendre	dar ré, apoiar alguém, retornar
back out	salir, retirarse, decidir lo contrario	sortir, changer d'avis	retirar, voltar atrás, faltar a uma promessa ou compromisso
have one's heart set on	anhelar, ansiar	avoir envie de, tenir à	desejar muito
buy up	adquirir, acaparar	faire l'achat total	comprar todo o estoque
buy out	comprar la parte de	acheter la part de	comprar a parte de
sell out	vender, liquidar	vendre, liquider	esgotar-se, liquidar, trair
catch on	popularizarse, darse cuenta, entender	devenir populaire, y être, comprendre	virar moda, entender

ENGLISH	SPANISH	FRENCH	PORTUGUESE
be cut out for	tener talento para	avoir l'étoffe de	ter talento para
throw out	echar, botar	jetter à la porte, rejeter	jogar fora, expulsar alguém, rejeitar (proposta, projeto de lei)
throw up	erigir, vomitar	ériger, vomir	erguer ou construir rapidamente, vomitar
clear up	aclarar, solucionar	s'éclaircir, clarifier, résoudre	esclarecer, clarear, melhorar (tempo)

Lesson 30

slow down	ir más despacio	ralentir	ir mais devagar, diminuir a velocidade
dry up	secarse completamente	sécher	secar
dry out	secarse poco a poco	dessécher	secar, enxugar, parar de beber
be up to (something)	tener algo entre manos	machiner, combiner	estar ocupado em, estar tramando algo
beat around the bush	andarse con rodeos	tourner autour du pot	falar ou responder com rodeios
come to an end	terminar, acabarse	se terminer	acabar, terminar
put an end to	darle fin a	faire cesser, mettre un terme à	acabar com algo, pôr fim a algo
get even with	vengarse	se venger	vingar-se de alguém
fool around	perder el tiempo, bromear	perdre son temps plaisanter	perder tempo, vadiar, brincar
look out on	dar a	donner sur	dar para, ter vista sobre
stir up	provocar, incitar	exciter, pousser à, agiter	provocar, instigar
take in	escuchar, engañar	voir, décevoir	visitar, diminuir, enganar, iludir

Lesson 31

go through	sufrir, consumir	souffrir, consumer	passar por, sofrer, gastar, chegar ao fim de
go without saying	estar sobre entendido	il va sans dire que	subentender-se, ser óbvio

ENGLISH	SPANISH	FRENCH	PORTUGUESE
put (someone) on	bromear, tomarle el pelo (a alguien)	faire marcher (quelqu'un)	brincar, enganar
keep one's head	mantener la calma	garder son sang froid	manter a calma
lose one's head	perder la cabeza	perdre la tête	perder a cabeça, perder o controle
narrow-minded	de mirar estrechas	à l'esprit étroit	de mentalidade estreita, tacanho
stand up	durar, dejar plantado	faire bon usage, résister, poser un lapin	durar, agüentar, dar o cano em alguém
get the better of	aventajar	l'emporter sur	vencer, levar a melhor
break loose	soltarse, zafarse	se détacher de, s'échapper, s'évader	soltar-se, escapar
on edge	ansioso, irritable	énervé	nervoso, ansioso, tenso
waste one's breath	perder el tiempo	perdre son temps	falar em vão, perder tempo em conversas
cut short	adelantar, reducir	couper court	reduzir, interromper

Lesson 32

ENGLISH	SPANISH	FRENCH	PORTUGUESE
step in	intervenir, entrar	intervenir, entrer	intervir, entrar
step down	retirarse, renunciar	démissionner	afastar-se, demitir-se
step on	apurarse	se dépêcher	apressar-se, acelerar
a steal	una ganga	une occasion	uma pechincha, negócio vantajoso
play up to	dar coba, adular	flatter	bajular
more or less	casi, más o menos	presque, plus ou moins	mais ou menos
screw up	echar a perder confundir	ruiner, gâter	confundir, estragar tudo
goof up	pifiar, fallar	faire une gaffe	dar uma mancada, dar um fora
go off the deep end	montar en cólera y hacer algo precipitadamente	s'emporter, s'emballer	perder a cabeça
lose one's touch	perder la maña	perdre la main ou la touche	perder o jeito de
under control	bajo control	avoir (quelque chose) bien en main	sob controle

ENGLISH	SPANISH	FRENCH	PORTUGUESE
drag one's heels/ feet	flatar a su deber	mettre peu d'entrain à	ser deliberadamente lerdo, vagaroso, mostrar-se relutante

Lesson 33

kick (some thing) around	debatir un asunto	ruminer, discuter	discutir, debater um assunto
on the ball	alerta, listo	alerte	estar ou ficar ligado, atento
make up	compensar, inventar, maquillarse	se rattraper, inventer, se maquiller	compensar, criar, inventar, maquilar-se, compor
make up with	reconciliarse	se réconcilier	fazer as pazes
pull together	calmarse	rassembler, se calmer	colher (informações), acalmar-se
be looking up	estar mejorando	être à la hausse, promettre	melhora, parecer promissor
kick the habit	dejar un vicio	se débarasser du vice	largar o vício
cover up	encubrir	dissimuler	encobrir algo
drop off	dormirse, entregar, bajar rápido	s'endormir, livrer, tomber	pegar no sono, deixar alguém, diminuir
turn over	poner al revés, transferir	reverser, transférer	virar algo do outro lado, capotar, transferir algo para alguém
go through channels	hacer algo debidamente	respecter, suivre la hiérarchie	seguir os canais competentes
last straw	el colmo	le comble	a última gota d'água

Lesson 34

get cold feet	acobardarse, rajarse	avoir la frousse	ficar com medo
trade in	canjear, cambiar	échanger	dar algo como parte do pagamento
face-to-face	cara a cara	face à face	cara a cara
be with (someone)	estar de parte de, acordar	être avec quelqu'un	concordar com, entender ou seguir o que alguém está dizendo

ENGLISH	SPANISH	FRENCH	PORTUGUESE
be with it	estar alerta, en forma	se mettre à la mode	estar atento, alerta
fall for	enamorarse, tragárselo, caer en la trampa	tomber amoureux de, se laisser prendre à	apaixonar-se, ser enganado por
it figures	por supuesto, claro	c'est logique ou normal	faz sentido
make (someone) tick	motivar a	motiver, pousser	motivar alguém
cover for	asumir los deberes de otra persona	couvrir, remplacer	substituir alguém, proteger alguém
give (someone) a break	darle oportunidad a alguien	donner une chance ou une opportunité	dar uma oportunidade a alguém, deixar alguém em paz
bow out	salirse	démissionner	retirar-se
stick it out	aguantar, soportar	tenir le coup	agüentar, tolerar

Lesson 35

rub it in	refregar por las narices	insister sur	insistir em assunto desagradável
rub the wrong way	caerle mal a alguien	prendre quelqu'un à rebrousse—poil	ofender ou irritar alguém
get a rise out of	causar enojo a alguien	mettre en colère	irritar, provocar alguém
hang around	quedarse a esperar	attendre	ficar esperando, ficar à toa
pick up the tab	pagar la cuenta	offrir l'addition	pagar as despesas, arcar com as despesas
by the way	de paso, incidentalmente	à propos, au fait	por falar nisso, a propósito
let slide	evitar una responsabilidad	négliger, laisser aller les choses	deixar passar, desinteressar-se de
search me	¡Que a mí no me pregunten!	ne pas avoir la moindre idée	Sei lá!
get off one's chest	desahogarse	déballer	desabafar, dizer o que sente
live it up	darse vida de rico	mener la belle vie	aproveitar a vida
liven up	animar	égayer	animar-se, alegrar algo
have a say/voice in	tener voz en algun asúnto	avoir voix au chapitre	ter voz ativa em algo

ENGLISH	SPANISH	FRENCH	PORTUGUESE
Lesson 36			
out of the question	ni hablar	hors de question	impossível, fora de cogitação
have to do with	tener que ver con	avoir quelque chose à voir avec	ter a ver com, dizer respeito a
check in	llegar a un hotel	s'inscrire sur le registre d'un hôtel	fazer o registro de entrada
check out	pagar la cuenta de un hotel	régler son compte en quittant un hôtel	fazer o resgistro de saída, investigar, examinar
take one at one's word	creer incondicionalmente	prendre quelqu'un au mot	levar alguém a sério, confiar em alguém
serve one's purpose	ser de utilidad, convenirle a	faire l'affaire	ser útil, vir a calhar
cop out	evadir una responsabilidad	renoncer à, eviter ses responsabilités	voltar atrás, faltar a uma promessa ou compromisso
line up	preparar algo o alguien	s'aligner, préparer	fazer fila, arranjar
lose one's cool	perder la calma	perdre son sang-froid	perder a calma
leave open	dejar pendiente	laisser en suspens	deixar pendente
miss the boat	perder una oportunidad	rater l'occasion	perder uma oportunidade
think up	inventar	inventer	inventar, criar
Lesson 37			
throw (someone) a curve	confundir, cogerlo a uno desprevenido	confondre, prendre au dépourvu	confundir, pegar alguém desprevenido
make waves	romper la calma, estorbar el orden	faire des histoires	perturbar a calma ou a ordem
carry on	continuar	continuer	continuar, levar avante, proceder de modo estranho
not on your life	ni hablar de eso	jamais de la vie	de forma alguma, nunca, nem por um decreto
cover ground	llevar mucho a cabo	couvrir beaucoup de terrain	cobrir uma matéria
throw the book at	castigar severamente	être strict ou dur	punir severamente
put one's foot in	meter la pata	mettre les pieds dans le plat	cometer uma gafe, dar um fora

ENGLISH	SPANISH	FRENCH	PORTUGUESE
be up for grabs	estar disponible, fácil de obtener	être disponible	estar disponível
show off	jactarse	crâner, faire parade de	mostrar-se, exibir-se
learn the ropes	aprender las rutinas	apprendre son affaire	aprender, assimilar a rotina
have under one's belt	tener (algo) controlado	avoir (quelque chose) contrôlé	ter emplacado algo
keep one's fingers crossed	ojalá que así sea	avoir bon espoir	ficar torcendo para que algo dê certo

Lesson 38

ENGLISH	SPANISH	FRENCH	PORTUGUESE
land on one's feet	caer de pie como un gato	retomber sur ses pieds	safar-se, dar um jeito
dish out	dar algo en abundancia, derrochar, dar a manos llenas	servir, critiquer	dar algo em grande quantidade, criticar alguém
get through to	hacer entender a alguien	faire comprendre à quelqu'un	fazer alguém entender algo
keep one's word	cumplir lo prometido	tenir sa parole	cumprir a palavra
be in over one's head	estar abrumado	être accablé dépassé	estar atolado de trabalho, estar acima da compreensão de alguém
ask for	merecer algún castigo o contrariedad	mériter une punition adversité	procurar problema, procurar sarna pra se coçar
be a far cry from	ser muy distinto	être très différent	ser muito diferente de
by all means	definitivamente	bien sûr	sem dúvida, certamente
get out from under	salir a flote	surmonter ses pertes	sair de situações financeiras difíceis
take the bull by the horns	enfrentarse con	être déterminé, décisif	enfrentar diretamente as dificuldades ou a situação
give (someone) a hand	echar una mano	donner un coup de mains	dar uma ajuda, dar uma mãozinha para alguém
give (someone) a big hand	aplaudir	applaudir chaudement	aplaudir efusivamente

ENGLISH	SPANISH	FRENCH	PORTUGUESE

Lesson 39

behind one's back	a espaldas de uno	derrière son dos, à son insu	por detrás, nas costas de alguém, em segredo
talk back to	protestar	rétorquer	responder a alguém (de maneira desrespeitosa)
be in	estar a la moda	être à la page	estar na moda, estar disponível, desocupado
be out	estar fuera de moda	hors de mode	estar fora de moda, não estar no trabalho ou em casa
draw the line at	definir el límite en	se refuser à	definir o limite, apontar o limite do que é aceitável
get out of line	desobedecer	désobéir	desobedecer, sair da linha
dry run	ensayo	faire des essais ou des épreuves	ensaio
play by ear	tocar algo de oído	jouer par oreille	tocar de ouvido
be in (someone's) shoes	estar en la posición de otro	être à la place d'un autre	colocar-se na situação de alguém
keep after	recordar constantemente	rappeler continuellement, harceler	ficar no pé, azucrinar
fix up	arreglar, concertar una cita	réparer, assigner un rendezvous	consertar, organizar, acertar (um encontro, uma viagem, etc.)
be had	ser engañado, timado, estafado	être roulé, trompé, dupé, volé	ser enganado

ANSWER KEY

Lesson 1

A. 1. b 2. b 3. a 4. b 5. c 6. a 7. c 8. b 9. c 10. b

B. turns off / right away / gets up / sooner or later / turns on / takes off / puts on

Lesson 2

A. 1. c 2. c 3. a 4. b 5. c 6. a 7. b 8. b 9. b 10. a

B. dress up / looking for / tired out / never mind / looking at / found out / spent . . . time /all along

Lesson 3

A. 1. a 2. c 3. b 4. b 5. b 6. a 7. c 8. b 9. c 10. a

B. by yourself / take out / all . . . long / on purpose / talk over / get along with / sit down

Lesson 4

A. 1. c 2. a 3. c 4. a 5. b 6. c 7. a 8. b 9. b 10. a

B. wait on / at all / so far / at least / take a walk / think . . . over

Lesson 5

A. 1. b 2. a 3. c 4. b 5. a 6. b 7. a 8. b 9. c 10. b

B. get back / in a hurry / make up my mind / gotten over / for the time being / put off

Lesson 6

A. 1. a 2. b 3. c 4. c 5. b 6. a 7. a 8. c 9. b 10. c

B. go on / have . . . time off / all of a sudden / hang out / make friends / hang up

Lesson 7

A. 1. c 2. b 3. a 4. a 5. c 6. c 7. c 8. b 9. b 10. a

B. had better / would rather / figure out / point out / think . . . of / in time to

Lesson 8

A. 1. b 2. a 3. c 4. b 5. a 6. c 7. b 8. c 9. a 10. b

B. worn out / over and over again / go out / throw . . . away / out of the question / have to do with / fallen in love

Lesson 9

A. 1. a 2. c 3. c 4. b 5. a 6. a 7. b 8. c 9. b 10. b

B. wake up / am used to / in no time / be in charge of / have a good time

Lesson 10

A. 1. b 2. c 3. b 4. b 5. a 6. b 7. c 8. a 9. b 10. a

B. get rid of / go with / make good time / first-rate / make a . . . impression / by heart / make sure

Lesson 11

A. 1. a 2. c 3. b 4. a 5. b 6. a 7. c 8. b 9. a 10. c

B. keep out / get through / do . . . over / from now on / keep away from / up to / find fault with / ill at ease / get carried away

Lesson 12

A. 1. b 2. a 3. c 4. a 5. c 6. c 7. a 8. a 9. b 10. a

B. broke out / burned down / for one thing / out of date / burned up *or* ticked off / as for / feel sorry for / stands to reason / up-to-date

Lesson 13

A. 1. a 2. a 3. b 4. c 5. c 6. c 7. a 8. a 9. b 10. c

B. turns out / have on / broke down / once in a blue moon / calls for / take for granted / comes to / take into account

Collocations

going / like / of the question / of control / free / funny / it / of date

Review: Lessons 1–13

A. 1. d   2. l   3. a   4. g   5. f   6. l   7. k   8. b   9. c   10. e   11. h
   12. j

B. 1. F   2. F   3. T   4. T   5. F   6. T   7. F   8. T   9. F   10. T   11. T
   12. F

C. 1. to look at   2. to look into   3. to look up   4. looked over   5. look
   for   6. Look out

D. 1. to take place   2. take hold of   3. take your time   4. took out   5. to
   take part in   6. to take into account   7. take turns   8. take off   9. to
   take a trip

E. 1. get rid of   2. got used to   3. to get over   4. to get on; get off
   5. get out of; get in   6. to get along with   7. gets up; gets to; gets back

Lesson 14

A. 1. c   2. a   3. b   4. a   5. c   6. c   7. a   8. b   9. b   10. a

Lesson 15

A. 1. c   2. c   3. a   4. b   5. a   6. c   7. a   8. c   9. b   10. c

Lesson 16

A. 1. b   2. c   3. c   4. b   5. b   6. b   7. c   8. c   9. b   10. a

Lesson 17

A. 1. a   2. b   3. a   4. c   5. a   6. c   7. a   8. b   9. b   10. a

Lesson 18

A. 1. c   2. a   3. a   4. a   5. b   6. b   7. c   8. b   9. a   10. c

Lesson 19

A. 1. b   2. a   3. b   4. b   5. c   6. a   7. a   8. b   9. b   10. c

Lesson 20

A. 1. c   2. a   3. b   4. b   5. a   6. b   7. c   8. b   9. a   10. b

Lesson 21

A. 1. b   2. a   3. b   4. c   5. c   6. a   7. b   8. b   9. a   10. c

Lesson 22

A. 1. a   2. c   3. b   4. a   5. b   6. c   7. b   8. a   9. b   10. a

Lesson 23

A. 1. c   2. b   3. b   4. c   5. b   6. a   7. a   8. c   9. b   10. c

Lesson 24

A. 1. c   2. c   3. b   4. a   5. a   6. b   7. b   8. c   9. b   10. c

Lesson 25

A. 1. c   2. c   3. a   4. a   5. b   6. b   7. c   8. a   9. c   10. a

Lesson 26

A. 1. b   2. c   3. a   4. a   5. b   6. c   7. a   8. b   9. b   10. c

Lesson 27

A. 1. c   2. a   3. b   4. b   5. c   6. b   7. b   8. a   9. a   10. c

Collocations

place / sides / the law / your pick / a habit / the story / care

Review: Lessons 14–27

A. 1. i   2. c   3. k   4. e   5. g   6. l   7. b   8. d   9. j   10. a   11. f
    12. h

B. 1. T   2. F   3. T   4. T   5. T   6. T   7. F   8. F   9. T   10. T   11. T
    12. T

C. 1. close call   2. called it a day   3. calls for   4. calls

D. 1. make a difference   2. to make fun of   3. made good time   4. make sense   5. to make do   6. make sure   7. make out   8. make . . . clear   9. to make the best of

E. 1. put away   2. put up with   3. put on   4. put out   5. put off   6. to put down   7. to put together

Collocations

quiet / in mind / it with / his name / to the subject / his throat / the change

Review: Lessons 28–39

A. 1. e   2. l   3. a   4. f   5. g   6. b   7. k   8. l   9. d   10. h   11. c   12. j

B. 1. T   2. F   3. T   4. F   5. T   6. T   7. F   8. F   9. F   10. T   11. F   12. T

C. 1. gave birth to   2. to give me a break   3. give and take   4. give me a hand   5. gave him/her a big hand   6. gave out   7. is giving off   8. gave up or gave in   9. give in

D. 1. to keep his head   2. to keep up with   3. to keep track of   4. to keep after   5. keep your word   6. keep in touch with   7. to keep away   8. to keep in mind   9. keep our fingers crossed

E. 1. went off   2. went over   3. touch and go   4. to go around   5. went through   6. go wrong   7. goes of the deep end   8. goes without saying   9. goes with

INDEX

The number refers to the page on which the idiom or collocation is first introduced. An (**R**) indicates an idiom that appears in a lesson as a related form.